This book should be returned to any branch of the
Lancashire County Library on or before the date shown

Lancashire County Library
Bowran Street
Preston PR1 2UX

Lancashire
County Council

www.lancashire.gov.uk/libraries

Follifoot Publishing Limited

First Published in Great Britain in 2009 by Follifoot Publishing Limited, The Cottage, Rudding Lane, Follifoot, Harrogate, North Yorkshire, HG3 1DQ. www.follifootpublishing.co.uk

For Heather and Louise

ISBN 978-0-9562468-0-6

The author and the publisher have made every effort to ensure that the information in this publication is accurate and as up-to-date as possible at the time of going to print. However, over the course of time details change and neither the author nor the publisher can accept any responsibility for any loss, injury or inconvenience experienced by any person or persons whilst using this book.

Walking is not an entirely risk-free activity and whilst the author and the publisher have made every reasonable effort to highlight potential risks neither can accept responsibility for loss, injury or damage, however occasioned, to any person or persons (including their property) undertaking the walk described in this book.

Book cover design by Gary Lawson (www.g1creative.co.uk)

Printed in England by MTP Media, The Sidings, Beezon Fields, Kendal, Cumbria, LA9 6BL

Contents

8100491608

Locator Map

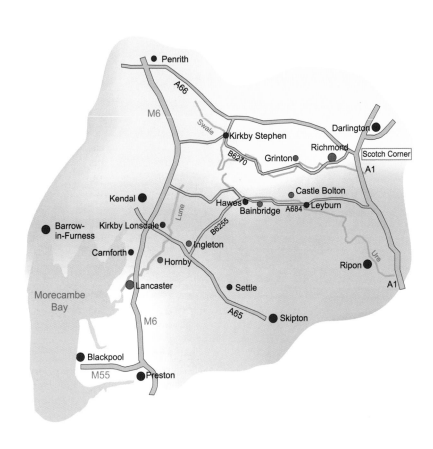

Mileage Chart

Lancaster to Richmond as the crow flies...50 miles (80.5km)

Lancaster to Richmond via classified roads..62 ½ miles (100.6km)

The Richmond Way..60 ½ miles (97.3km)

The Richmond Way is the name given by the author to a 60 ½ mile-long (97.3km) linear walk starting from the main gate of Lancaster Castle and ending below the great keep of Richmond Castle in North Yorkshire. The walk encompasses sections of the lower Lune Valley, the limestone country around Ingleborough and Whernside and the central and northern valleys of the Yorkshire Dales National Park. The route is almost entirely along field, woodland and riverside paths, ancient tracks and quiet country lanes. The Richmond Way does not exist in a formal sense; it does not have the status of an officially recognised trail such as the Pennine Way or the Offa's Dyke Path and the walker will not find any reference to it on waymarkers or signposts. Nevertheless, the route, devised and tested by the author over a number of years, is along public rights of way that in the main are reasonably well waymarked. The clear, easy to follow route directions in this guidebook, supported by 58 maps dedicated to the route, should, when supplemented by the relevant OS 1:25 000 map, make navigation relatively straightforward.

A strong walker could complete the walk within two days, though more realistically an average walker even if accompanied by children should be able to complete the walk inside five days. Some people may prefer to complete the walk over a longer timeframe, weeks or even months, by completing individual sections as and when the opportunity arises.

The following is a brief description of the route taken by the Richmond Way:

The Lower Lune Valley

From the historic city of Lancaster, with its hilltop castle, 15th-century priory church, 18th-century quay and warehouses and many fine bridges, the route follows the River Lune (which has its source in the Howgill Fells in Cumbria and flows in a south-westerly direction between the Lake District and the Yorkshire Dales) and its tributary, the Greta, upstream to Ingleton in North Yorkshire.

The route passes through or close to the ancient villages of Halton, with its Viking Cross displaying both Christian and pagan symbols, Aughton, renowned for its great pudding festivals, Gressingham, an attractive village above the Lune, Hornby, with its unusual 16th-century octagonal church tower, Arkholme, whose tiny stone church is built alongside a Norman motte,

Melling, with its handsome houses and Burton-in-Lonsdale, whose famous son is the poet Laurence Binyon.

The stretch of river from Aughton to Arkholme is a paradise for ornithologists and, depending on the time of year, various species of waterfowl (ducks, geese and swans) can be seen along with wading birds (redshanks, oystercatchers and herons). In summer, wagtails and swallows put on an amazing aerobatic display in their quest to catch insects above the river, and just occasionally the walker may catch sight of an electric-blue kingfisher as it flashes up the Lune.

Limestone country

At Ingleton, famous for its glens and waterfalls, the route leaves the lowlands behind and enters an upland landscape dominated by limestone and the iconic Yorkshire mountains of Ingleborough and Whernside. The surrounding hillsides are etched deep with limestone scars created by retreating ice formed during the last Ice Age. The route from Ingleton to the head of Ribblesdale via Scales Moor traverses spectacular limestone pavements whose weathered crevices have been colonised by (and occasionally rare) woodland plants. The higher sections of the route are lined by curiously shaped potholes.

At Ribblehead the Richmond Way passes beneath the most famous viaduct in the north of England whose 24 arches carry the Settle—Carlisle Railway on a course that crosses the high moors of the central Pennines. Just beyond Ribblehead the route adopts an old Roman road (see Appendix One: Historical Setting) which it follows to Wether Fell via Cam End and Dodd Fell Hill. This section of the Richmond Way is over some of the most exposed and isolated moors and fells in England. The route reaches 590 metres (1935ft) at its highest point and for 10 exhilarating miles sustains a height above 305 metres (1000ft).

The Central and Northern Valleys of the Yorkshire Dales National Park

The Richmond Way enters Raydale, a secluded tributary valley of Wensleydale, where farmers have grazed their cattle on the fells since time immemorial. Spreading across the valley floor is Semer Water, a jewel of a lake, surrounded by a magnificent bowl of hills. The route explores the lower reaches of Raydale before entering Wensleydale, the largest of the Yorkshire Dales. The route passes through the villages of Bainbridge, with its huge sloping green and Askrigg, with its Grade I listed church and a main street lined with fine Georgian houses. From Askrigg the Richmond Way seeks out an old drovers' road which it follows to Castle Bolton, whose linear green is dominated at one end by a medieval fortress where Mary Queen of Scots was imprisoned by Queen Elizabeth I. From Castle Bolton the route strikes out in a northerly direction in order to avoid MOD firing ranges, which cover vast swathes of moorland between Richmond and Leyburn. After crossing Redmire Moor the route enters Swaledale via the summit of Greets Hill.

The final leg of the journey to Richmond starts from the ancient village of Grinton and follows the River Swale downstream to Marrick Priory before exploring the old lead mining villages of Marrick and Marske. Just beyond Marske the route follows a delightful fellside terrace above the looping Swale. On the outskirts of Richmond the route rejoins the Swale which it follows downstream to Richmond Bridge. A final crossing of the Swale is made before the route enters the market town of Richmond where it terminates below the great keep of Richmond Castle. Richmond is a romantic and historic town (predating all other towns bearing the same name) replete with an 11th-century castle, a graceful 15th-century Gothic-style bell tower, the largest market square in England, a former French quarter, attractive Georgian buildings, including the oldest Georgian theatre in England.

Using this Guidebook

Information panels

This guidebook divides the route into seven sections broadly equating to areas sharing similar physical characteristics, though there is a degree of overlap. The longest section is 13 ¾ miles (22.1km) and the shortest 4 ¾ miles (7.6km). Each section is introduced by an information panel showing its distance, the approximate time to complete the section (though clearly this will depend on frequency of stops, level of fitness and prevailing weather conditions), the nature of the terrain, a brief description of the route, a route-overview map and the relevant OS 1:25 000 map(s) covering the section.

The information panel also includes facilities (generally referenced by location, not business name) along the route, that is accommodation, shops, post offices banks, chemists, public houses, restaurants, cafes and tea rooms. Brief details about public transport operating within the section are also included.

Route directions

To facilitate navigation each section provides a detailed description of the route supported by dedicated route maps. However, the reader should always bear in mind that the directions and route maps (which are not to scale and lack detail such as field boundaries and contours) will be of little use in fog, heavy mist, low cloud or driving snow, where you cannot see more than a few metres ahead let alone a stile in the far corner of a field or an isolated barn or a plantation of trees in the middle distance. Therefore a compass and the relevant OS 1:25 000 map (and a knowledge of their use) are essential items. On the higher sections of the walk you may need to consider an escape route in the event of being overtaken by inclement weather, and in these circumstances the relevant OS 1:25 000 map will be essential. It should also be recognised that landmarks change over time — farms, and all too frequently barns, are converted into residential dwellings, hedges uprooted, trees felled, old stiles replaced by metal gates, walls demolished, rights of way diverted. The current trend (which is to be welcomed though it can make nonsense of route directions) is for rights of way to be re-routed around the perimeter of farms and away from farmyards where livestock are housed.

Heritage and historical setting

Apart from magnificent scenery the Richmond Way is rich in archaeological sites, ancient monuments, prehistoric fields and settlements, ancient tracks and roads, medieval castles, motte and bailey earthworks, historic churches, monastic remains, manor houses, ancient bridges, an 18th-century aqueduct, water-powered mills, turnpike roads, streets and squares lined with Georgian houses, Victorian railway engineering at its zenith. These historical features of the landscape add an interesting dimension to the walk and are highlighted throughout this guidebook. Each section also provides historical background information on towns and villages en route to Richmond.

The genesis of the walk described in this guidebook can be traced to the military ambitions of a great Roman general who ruled Britain nearly 2,000 years ago and the reader is referred to Appendix One which provides the historical setting for the walk.

Geology of the Yorkshire Dales

Whilst it is outside the scope of this guidebook to provide anything but a brief description of the main geological features found in the Yorkshire Dales, the reader may find the information in Appendix Two adds to the enjoyment of the walk.

Safety Information

Weather and equipment

If this walk was transplanted to North America at the same latitude the walker would find him-or herself at least a 1,000 miles north of New York. In fact, the southern tip of Alaska lies on the same latitude as the walk! Of course, thanks to the Gulf Stream warming the seas around our island, Britain has a breezy, temperate climate. But away from the coast and with even quite modest increases in altitude, the weather conditions can be extremely changeable both in summer and winter. Even in early spring or late autumn it is not uncommon to experience on the fells (and not infrequently at lower levels) raw, damp, cold days with a penetrating wind and temperatures close to or below freezing point. The more exposed areas of the route, that is Ingleton to Semer Water and Castle Bolton to Grinton, should not be undertaken by inexperienced fell walkers in winter, early spring or late autumn.

All walkers should be properly equipped with waterproofs, warm clothing, appropriate headgear (winter for warmth and summer for shade) and a good pair of walking boots suitable for the fells. Walkers should carry with them liquid refreshment (in summer dehydration can present a serious danger) and emergency rations, a first-aid kit, a high-factor sun cream, a torch, a whistle, a lightweight survival bag, a mobile phone, though there are black spots along the route, a watch, a compass and the relevant OS 1:25 000 map.

Always check the weather forecast before setting out, but above all know your limitations and be prepared to turn back should the weather deteriorate.

Sink holes, shake holes and pot holes, disused mine shafts and peat hags

All the above are a common feature of the Yorkshire Dales particularly the upland limestone areas. Pot holes, sinks holes and shake holes are particularly common between Ewes Top and Ribblehead. Holes in the ground are potentially dangerous and even a cursory investigation of them is not advised. The summit plateau of Wether Fell is covered in potentially dangerous peat hags. Unfenced disused mine shafts present a potential danger between Castle Bolton and Grinton. In these areas, especially, do not stray from the designated route (or other rights of way), keep dogs under control, and at all times watch where you plant your feet!

Livestock

There are very few areas along the route where you will not encounter livestock, mainly sheep and cattle. Wherever cattle are present there are added risks to the walker owing to their size and weight. In the presence of cattle keep dogs on a lead. Be extra vigilant in the presence of cows with calves. Never come between a cow and her calf. Dairy cattle (unless with calves) generally are more docile than beef cattle which are far more inquisitive and will gallop across the field to greet you before sliding to a dramatic halt within centimetres of your feet. Remain calm but always watchful. Crossing a pasture containing cattle, when there is thunder in the vicinity, is potentially dangerous.

Bulls are another potential risk though possibly not as great as cows with calves. The law relating to the keeping of bulls in fields crossed by public rights of way is anything but straightforward. Farmers by law must not place *dairy* bulls over 10 months old in a field crossed by a public right of way. But they can put any other breed over 10 months old in the field provided it is accompanied by cows or heifers and provided the bull does not have a temperamental disposition! No one in their right mind is going to investigate whether the bull in the far corner of the field is one of the permitted exceptions. Just give the bull a wide berth. Incidentally, when a bull has been taken from a field signs denoting its presence should be removed or securely covered. There are landowners who observe this requirement but there are others who do not in the belief that the notice will dissuade walkers from lawfully crossing their land. If you encounter this problem report the matter to the local Rights of Way Office.

Distance: 9 ¾ miles (15.6km)

Walking Time: 5 hours approximately

Terrain: Easy walking throughout the route but care should be taken on riverside paths particularly after rain where exposed tree roots present a potential hazard.

Map: 1:25 000 OS Explorer 0L41— Forest of Bowland & Ribblesdale

Route at a Glance:

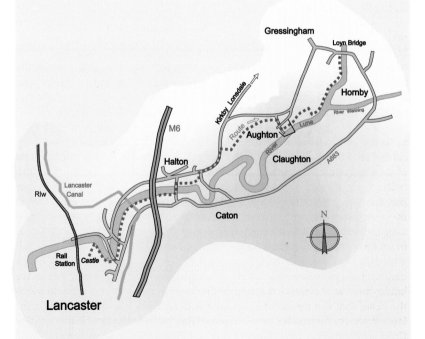

Route Overview: From Lancaster Castle the route descends to the south bank of the River Lune via St George's Quay where it joins a disused railway track, sections of which have been incorporated into the River Lune Millennium Park as a path and cycleway. The route adopts the path and cycleway which follows the river upstream passing under Skerton Bridge, alongside Skerton Weir, under Rennie's Aqueduct and beneath the M6 viaduct at Halton.

At Halton the route crosses the Lune and proceeds along the north bank of the river to the Crook O' Lune where it turns away from the river bank in favour of higher ground en route to Aughton. From Aughton the route rejoins the Lune which it follows upstream through broad riverside pastures and old watercourses to Loyn Bridge (Hornby).

The route is exceptionally well signposted to the Crook O' Lune but waymarking is indifferent thereafter.

Accommodation: Lancaster offers a good selection of hotels to suit most budgets including inns with rooms, guest houses and B&Bs. A country house hotel overlooks the Crook O' Lune, Caton. NB Lancaster has no youth hostel.

Cafes, restaurants and tea rooms: Lancaster has an excellent selection of eateries. A locally renowned snack bar with selected opening days during the winter is located in the Crook O' Lune car park.

Tourist Information Centre: Lancaster

Post Offices: Lancaster, Caton and Hornby

Village Shops: Halton, Caton and Hornby

Chemists: Lancaster

Public Toilets: Lancaster and Crook O' Lune

Rail Services: Lancaster is on the West Coast Main Line with frequent direct services to London and Scotland and regular direct services to Manchester, Preston, Leeds and Barrow-in-Furness.

Bus Services: Lancaster, National Express. Local services to outlying villages including Halton, Caton, Hornby, Gressingham, Wennington, Burton-in-Lonsdale, Kirkby Lonsdale, Ingleton and (infrequently) Melling.

Castle Park — Georgian Lancaster

18th-century warehouses converted into modern offices

Dalton Square — Victorian Lancaster

Lancaster

Lancaster is situated within the north-west corner of Lancashire, just five miles from the Irish Sea. The eastern fringe of the city is flanked by the Forest of Bowland and to the south are the flat lowlands of the Lancashire plain. To the north-west of the city, beyond the sands and mud flats of Morecambe Bay, are the mountains of the Lake District, and, forming a natural barrier in the north-east, are the Howgill Fells and the mountains of the Yorkshire Dales.

Roman Garrison

The history of Lancaster is inextricably linked to the River Lune. The Romans, recognising the strategic importance of the Lune, built in 80 AD (circa) a fort on a hill-top overlooking the river. A civilian settlement of merchants and shopkeepers grew up alongside the Roman fort that eventually gave Lancaster its name "fort by the Lune".

For the next 300 years the small town prospered until the garrison was closed in 407 AD following the withdrawal of Roman soldiers from Britain.

Middle Ages

In 1150 (circa) the Normans built on the site of the Roman fortification a huge stone keep which replaced an earlier wooden structure erected shortly after the Norman Conquest.

The Millennium Suspension Bridge spanning the tidal Lune

King John enlarged the castle in the early 13th-century by adding curtain walls, towers and a huge gateway. In 1193 Richard the Lionheart granted a charter to the townspeople of Lancaster to hold a weekly market and annual fair.

Castle Park, Lancaster

Maritime Trade

Lancaster remained a quiet market town until its port began to develop rapidly during the 18th-century, when Lancaster was second only to Liverpool in transatlantic trade. Ships returned from the American and Caribbean colonies laden with sugar, rum, cotton and mahogany. However, there was a sinister and altogether darker side to this lucrative trade: the involvement of local merchants in the notorious slave trade.

Georgian Town

There lies at the very heart of the city a stylish Georgian town largely borne out of Lancaster's maritime past. Many of the elegant town houses built by wealthy merchants and local gentry in the 18th-century still survive. During this period of prosperity the old Town Hall, Shire Hall, Skerton Bridge, the Lancaster Canal and St George's Quay were constructed.

Victorian Lancaster

The industrialisation of Lancaster took place in the 19th-century. Cotton was a major industry but it did not dominate the town to the extent it did in other parts of Lancashire. During this period St Peter's Catholic cathedral, the Ashton Memorial and the new Town Hall in Dalton Square were built.

St Peter's Cathedral, Lancaster

Our walk to Richmond starts below the twin-towered gatehouse adjoining Lancaster Castle. From the gatehouse turn left into Castle Park and proceed in a clockwise direction around the perimeter of the castle. Castle Park is a graceful corner of old Lancaster with its tree-lined green and elegant two-and three-storey Georgian houses. No 2 Castle Park is the former George Fox School. George Fox, founder of the Quakers, was imprisoned in Lancaster Castle for two years. Further round the castle complex is Shire Hall recognisable by its Gothic-style architecture.

Lancaster

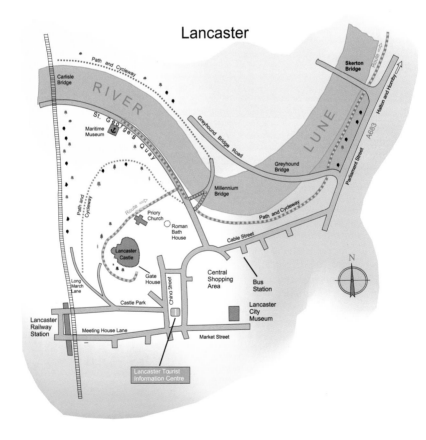

Lancaster Castle

Lancaster Castle occupies a prominent hilltop site overlooking Lancaster and the River Lune. The stone castle replaced an earlier wooden structure built in 1093 (circa) by Roger of Poitou, a loyal supporter of William I.

Lancaster Castle is a Grade I listed building and is owned by HM Queen Elizabeth II in right of the Duchy of Lancaster.

The castle consists of a group of buildings of differing architectural styles built between 1150 and 1821. The oldest building is the 12th-century Norman keep.

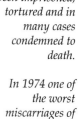
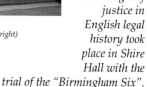

Norman keep (centre) and Shire Hall (right)

were transported to Australia. Lancaster Castle has always served as both a court and a castle, a role it still fulfils at the time of writing.

Throughout the ages many prisoners have suffered and died here in barbarous and harrowing conditions. Roman Catholics, Protestants, Quakers and those accused of witchcraft have been imprisoned, tortured and in many cases condemned to death.

In 1974 one of the worst miscarriages of justice in English legal history took place in Shire Hall with the trial of the "Birmingham Six".

Architecturally the most interesting building is Shire Hall, a semi-polygonal structure designed in the Gothic Revival style by Thomas Harrison and Joseph Gandy and which houses an 18th-century court-room from where thousands of convicts, for the pettiest of crimes,

Parts of the castle, including Shire Hall with its fine display of heraldic shields, are open to the public with restrictions when the Crown Court is in Session. Unfortunately, neither the Norman keep nor the John O' Gaunt gatehouse are open to the public at any time.

The twin-towered gatehouse

From Shire Hall head towards
the Priory Church of St Mary.
On reaching the church tower
look back towards the castle for
the best view of the Norman
keep which so far has largely
been hidden from sight. The keep
at 20 metres (98ft) is the tallest
building within the castle
complex.

The Gothic-style Shire Hall

*The gatehouse was built during the
reign of Henry IV whose father, the
first Duke of Lancaster (1340—99)
was immortalised by Shakespeare as
"Old John of Gaunt, time honoured
Lancaster". The current Duke of
Lancaster is HM Queen Elizabeth II.
Amongst the masonry of the
gatehouse can be seen a statute of
John O' Gaunt.*

From the tower take the signposted path leading down to St
George's Quay. The path
provides a good view of Carlisle
Bridge, which carries the West
Coast Main Line across the Lune,
and on a clear day Morecambe
Bay with the mountains of the
Lake District rising beyond. In a
field on the right-hand side of the
path (marked by a signpost) are
the remains of a partially
excavated Roman Bath House
and fragments of a 4th-century
fort wall.

Elegant Georgian houses facing Castle Green

After a short distance descend a flight of stone steps, cross a cycleway and pass in front of a fine row of Victorian stone built cottages. After a second flight of stone steps the path emerges onto St George's Quay, which, until the recent construction of a massive concrete wall to prevent tidal surges from breaching the quay, was a pleasant tree-lined promenade and the most attractive spot along the tidal river. Turn left and walk forward until you reach the Custom House (now a Maritime Museum) designed by Richard Gillow of the famous cabinet-making family.

The Priory Church

The Priory Church is a late medieval building with an 18th-century tower originally forming a separate structure before being connected to the main building. The remains of a

St. George's Quay, Lancaster

Roman Basilica lie beneath the church's foundations. The priory was closed by Henry VIII in 1539 only to be reincarnated as the Parish Church of Lancaster the following year. The Priory Church is a Grade I listed building. Inside are many interesting features including some remarkable 14th-century wooden choir stalls.

Retrace your steps towards the Millennium Suspension Bridge passing on the way a terrace of old, fishermen's stone cottages. Do not pass under the arches of the old railway viaduct but walk onto the suspension bridge and on joining the main pathway turn right towards the viaduct. On reaching the south bank bear left (signposted Halton and Caton).

From here to Halton our route mainly follows a dismantled

St George's Quay

This quiet quay was once a hive of activity where tall masted ships unloaded their cargoes of sugar, cotton, rum and mahogany from the West Indies and American colonies. Many of the tall, narrow sandstone warehouses fronting the river have been converted into fashionable loft-style apartments and offices.

Old Fishermen's cottages

railway line, sections of which have been incorporated into the River Lune Millennium Park, a nine-mile network of footpaths, cycleways and bridleways stretching along the north and south banks of the Lune interspersed with modern works of art.

The Palladian Custom House

Continue along the riverside pathway using the subway to cross the busy approach road to Greyhound Bridge. On emerging from the subway continue along the pathway crossing an area of open parkland known as Green Ayre.

The eye-catching Millennium Bridge opened in 2001

Green Ayre

Green Ayre has over a long number of years seen many commercial activities which at first flourished and then waned—a water-powered corn mill, a shipyard which built ships for trade with the West Indies and more recently a railway station. Today there is no discernible evidence that any of these activities ever took place.

Pass under Skerton Bridge designed by Thomas Harrison and opened in 1787, and continue forward passing Skerton Weir which marks the end of the Lune estuary tidal reach. The weir was built to stop tidal salt water from flowing upstream but not salmon or sea trout, for built into the centre of the weir is one of the largest fish passes in Europe.

The close proximity of industrial works to the pathway does little

Millennium Bridge

The Millennium Bridge, opened in 2001, provides a new crossing of the Lune for pedestrians and cyclists. There have been bridges on this site since Roman times. The first medieval bridge was made from wood but due to high maintenance costs was replaced by a four-arched stone structure during the 15th century. This bridge was eventually demolished after the opening of Skerton Bridge in 1787, though its foundations can still be seen at low tide.

Greyhound Bridge

to enhance the attractiveness of this section of the walk but despair not, for coming into view is an 18th-century architectural wonder: Rennie's Aqueduct carrying the former Preston to Kendal canal high above the Lune. The aqueduct was completed in 1797 to the designs of John Rennie who also designed London and Waterloo bridges across the Thames.

Rennie's Aqueduct

Between Skerton Weir and the aqueduct is an observation platform built out into the river providing splendid views both upstream towards the aqueduct and downstream towards the weir.

Pass under the aqueduct and walk forward passing the rear of

Alternative route to Halton

The aqueduct tow path and a right of way along the north bank of the river provide an alternative (but scenically less attractive) route to Halton. To gain the tow path turn right at the viaduct (path signposted Caton Road) and close to an electricity pylon a steep flight of steps leads to the tow path, cross the river and drop down the steps on your left. At the

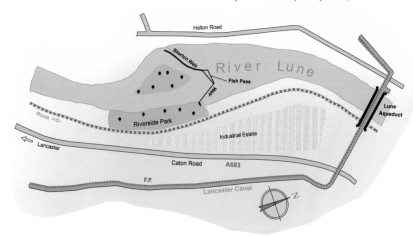

Skerton Bridge designed by Thomas Harrison

riverbank turn left and follow the riverside path passing through a territorial army training camp. Despite appearances to the contrary there is a right of way through the camp. The path eventually emerges where the Halton road passes underneath the M6 motorway. Turn right, pass under the motorway bridge and follow the pavement on your right which leads directly to the village.

The author's route can be rejoined at Mill Lane by the old Toll Bridge.

the Holiday Inn. 200 metres beyond the hotel on your left-hand side is a waymarked path which leads down to the riverbank. Take this path which follows the Lune upstream and makes a pleasant change from tarmac bashing. Pass underneath

the impressive M6 viaduct with its huge, graceful single concrete arch spanning the River Lune. The path now crosses a pleasant open field with delightful views across the river to picturesque houses with well-tendered gardens sloping down to the

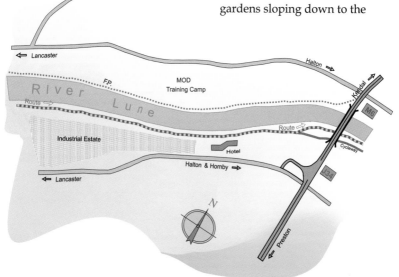

M6 viaduct at Halton

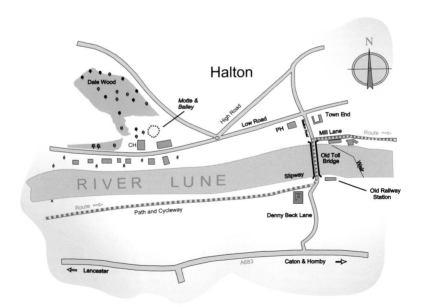

Lune. Standing on higher ground is St Wilfrid's Church with its medieval perpendicular tower and slightly to the right and rear of the church is a motte and bailey. The top of the motte is recognisable by its distinctive white flagpole. Below the church is Halton Hall though the original building has largely been subsumed into a relatively modern dwelling. The incessant roar of motorway traffic intrudes into what otherwise is an idyllic picture of riparian harmony and grace.

Walk to the end of the field and after passing through a kissing

Viking cross at Halton inscribed with both pagan and Christian symbols

gate rejoin the main pathway which leads to a car park. Continue to the end of the car park, turn left and follow the road down to an old toll bridge.

The Lune at Halton with St Wilfrid's Church standing on higher ground above the river

Halton

Halton is situated on the north bank of the Lune. A settlement has existed here since the 8th-century and in Saxon times Halton was a more important place than its close neighbour, Lancaster.

St Wilfrid's Church, Halton

The motte and bailey castle, of which only the earth works remain, was constructed in the late 11th-century by the Normans.

In the shadow of the motte and bailey stands St Wilfrid's Church built in 1792 but the tower dates from the 16th-century. The earliest known church on this site was built in 1067. A large Viking cross inscribed with both pagan and Christian symbols and dating from 1000 can be seen in the churchyard.

A tranquil stretch of the Lune at Halton

Cross the river taking care as both pedestrians and motorists share a narrow roadway. The bridge was opened in 1913 linking the village of Halton with its railway station on the south bank of the Lune.

After the bridge turn right onto Mill Lane and follow the road as it passes to the right of a modern development of riverside apartments en route to Forge Bank Weir. The weir can be reached by alternative routes —

the more interesting of the two being the one that hugs the river bank (but may be impassable when the river is running high) and passes alongside architectural relics of old mills.

The other route continues along Mill Lane which runs 50 metres or so above the riverside path. Both the lower and higher routes eventually converge at Forge Bank Weir. The upstream path circumvents the weir before dropping down to regain the riverbank. The vestiges of

Halton's industrial past are left behind as the path enters a more pastoral landscape.

Cross an open field at the end of which a footbridge leads into a beech wood which in late spring is teeming with bluebells. The path narrows as it climbs the steep riverside bank before leaving the wood via a kissing gate admitting to Low Road. Turn left (unless visiting the local beauty spot at the Crook O' Lune in which case turn right) and

quiet lane through pleasant open parkland above the Lune.

Across the river lies the ancient village of Caton with its 18th-century cotton mill and rising above the valley floor are the wild and desolate moors of the Forest of Bowland, a designated Area of Outstanding Natural

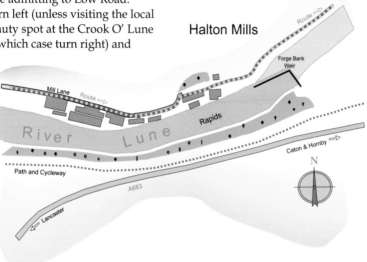

follow the pavement path for 200 metres. At the point where the road bends sharply leftwards a tarmac lane leads off to the right, close to a cattle grid sign. Cross the road with care and after the cattle grid follow the unenclosed

Beauty. Unbelievably, the eye-catching wind turbines whirling away on Caton Moor are sited on land included within the designation!

Cross a second cattle grid. The

lane now begins to rise steeply requiring a little exertion, although the splendid Scots pines bordering the lane make for a pleasant diversion of interest. On the skyline ahead is Yorkshire's most recognisable mountain, Ingleborough, with its flat-topped plateau, and once thought to be the highest mountain in England.

On your right, just coming into

Crook O' Lune

The Crook O' Lune is a local beauty spot providing wonderful views across the Lune Valley. The huge looping bend in the river was dramatically captured in a painting by the great romantic landscape painter, JMW Turner. Both William Wordsworth and Thomas Gray praised the lovely view. Three

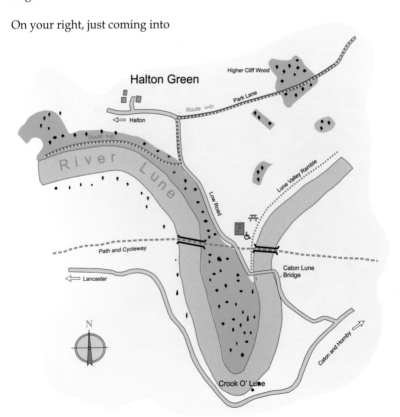

masonry bridges——one road and two disused railway——cross the Lune above the neck of the Crook. The two railway bridges are now part of the River Lune Millennium Park and can be crossed on foot. Both provide stunning views of the Lune far below.

Caton Lune Bridge

view are a jumble of old stone buildings comprising Halton Park. 200 metres beyond the driveway to Halton Park a finger post on your right supported by an informal sign directs to Hawkshead Farm, Windhover House and Kestral Cottage. At this point leave the road and follow a farm track on your right. In spring the dappled woodland bank alongside the farm track plays host to great swathes of bluebells. Spring comes early to this corner of Lancashire, which is warmed by the Gulf Stream, and the light, more intensive than further inland, augments the natural azure of the bluebells to breathtaking effect.

The River Lune near Caton

The farm track passes two dwellings on your right with a whitewashed farmhouse immediately ahead. 50 metres from the farmhouse on your left-hand side is an easily missed stile. If you find you are able to read the date above the farmhouse door (for those of a curious disposition it is 1683) then you need to beat a hasty retreat for you are on private property.

Cross the stile on your left and make a right diagonal crossing of the pasture aiming for a waymark that is just visible above a group of trees. The faint path circumvents the farm outbuildings and leads to a wire fence backed by a stone wall. A stile leads into a large pasture.

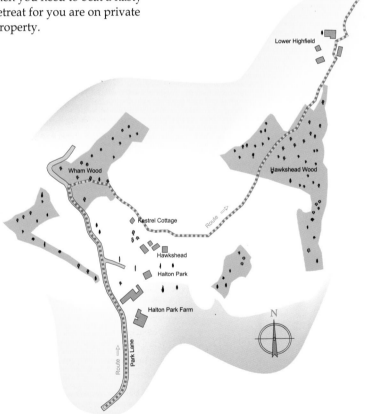

Cross the top of the pasture, which is bounded by a hawthorn hedge, and at the point where the hedge turns a corner and runs away northwards leave the hedge and strike out in a beeline towards a large gate leading into a wood on the opposite side of the pasture.

Enter the wood via a kissing gate and follow the somewhat boggy woodland path through the wood. Leave the wood via a second kissing gate and cross a small stream.

Now head towards a cluster of farm buildings. Pass through a metal gate and follow a broad track which leads to a three-storey farmhouse. Keep to the left of a barn (the right of way is waymarked) and pass through a second metal gate and locate a waymark just beyond the farm buildings. Pass through a third

Sweet violet

gate (the final one in the series), bear left and follow a wire fence around the perimeter of the farm. A helpful finger post directs to a metal gate in the far corner of the pasture. Initially aim for the gate but divert to a ladder stile located to the right of the gate. Cross over the stile and head towards the next farm. A wire fence on your left gives way to a dressed-stone wall which in a municipal park would make a handsome feature but in this pastoral landscape looks somewhat incongruous.

Follow the wall down to the farm passing through a metal gate. Keep to the right of the farm outbuildings and cross a stile next to a wooden gate. Head towards the front of a farm cottage and take a few steps into the farmyard. On your left there

Wild garlic

is a large outbuilding with a faded red door. Opposite the red door a cobbled path runs parallel to the gable end of the farm cottage. Follow this path to a stone gap stile next to an old chapel on your right and after crossing the stile aim for a waymark just beyond the farm track. Pass through a gate and follow the path as it passes in front of a farmhouse. Immediately ahead is a stile leading into a paddock where farm animals of the kind adored by children roam around. Aim

Two inquisitive little fellows

for a waymark located on the far side of the paddock. Leave the paddock via a stile and follow a faint path running alongside a hawthorn hedge on your left.

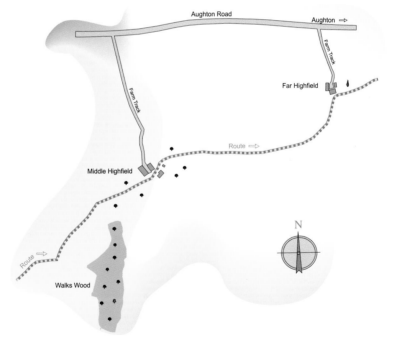

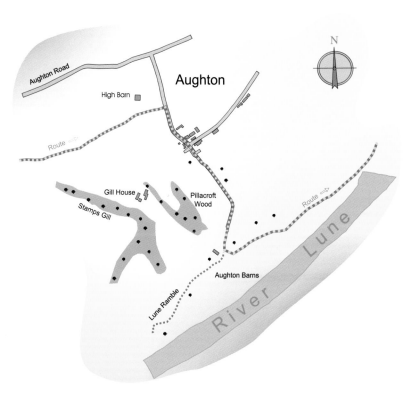

There can be no mistaking the next farm en route to our next objective, Aughton, as it lies in the shadow of a highly conspicuous telecom mast. On nearing the farm locate a wooden stile slightly to the right of the farmhouse. Take the stile into the next field and bear half-right towards an isolated hut in the middle of the field. The path dips into a shallow gill where a footbridge provides a dry crossing of a small stream.

The next waymarked stile is quite difficult to spot from a distance. From the footbridge make a right diagonal crossing of the field aiming for a clump of gorse on the far side but diverting to a ladder stile. Cross the stile into the adjoining field and once again make a right diagonal crossing aiming this time for a metal gate.

Gritstone cottages with stone mullion windows are a hallmark of Aughton

In late spring, before the mowers get to work, this meadow is ablaze with wild flowers. On the northern skyline are the Howgills, where amongst the fellside slopes the infant Lune springs to life. The main peaks of the Yorkshire Dales lie to the right of the Howgills. At the foot of the broad slopping meadow the Lune, now a mature river, is slipping effortlessly away towards the southern tip of Morecambe Bay where it will disgorge its waters. Two or three fields away Aughton, a shy, timeless settlement, is slowly revealing itself. This is rural Lancashire at its most picturesque.

Next to the metal gate is the penultimate stile before the Aughton road. Follow the faint path across the last pasture and after negotiating the metal ladder stile turn right and walk down the hill into Aughton. All roads in Aughton lead to a

Aughton

Aughton is a farming village standing some 200 metres above the steep northern bank of the Lune. The village comprises clusters of picturesque grit stone houses and barns. Many of the dwellings have stone mullion windows.

Time passes slowly in Aughton but once every 21 years the village throws off its torpor and springs to life. Folk from every corner of north Lancashire and surrounding areas invade the village for the great Pudding Festival. The origins of the festival lie in basket making. Long ago willows were collected from the riverbed and boiled in a huge cauldron. It was suggested in 1782 that the cauldron would make a wonderful plum pudding....and so it did! Look around the village and you may spot one of the giant pudding basins used in one the festivals.

Looking towards Loyn Bridge

small triangular green with a wooden seat, an ideal spot for spreading out one's map and taking refreshment before embarking on the next section of the walk.

From the green walk down the steep, high-banked lane towards the river (signposted cul-de-sac). At the foot of the bank on your right two adjoining stone cottages are set at right angles to the lane. Opposite the cottage closest to the lane is a waymarked stile alongside a ditch. Cross the ditch and enter a riverside field. The field contains what at first sight appear to be grave headstones set in alignment. The stones are in fact boundary markers dating from Saxon or, possibly, Norman times.

Cross the field in a north-easterly direction. Next to a metal gate a stile leads into the next field. The faint path crosses two further fields before reaching the northern bank of the Lune. Follow the Lune upstream. Sheep graze nonchalantly on the grassy embankment above the river. Shortly the path enters Great Close Wood. In spring

Springtime in the Lune Valley

Crow Wood

Path to Gressingham

Route

River Wenning

High Barn

The Snab

River Lune

Wild Carr
Wood

N

Route

Great Close
Wood

drifts of bluebells cascade down
the woodland banks towards the
river. In places the path through
the wood is steep and narrow
and comes perilously close to the
water's edge.

Leave the wood via a stile and
continue along the riverside path
through semi-open terrain until

Drifts of bluebells along the banks of the Lune

Looking down the Lune near Hornby

you reach what appears to be the confluence of two rivers. But which one of the two channels is the Lune? Surprisingly, it is not the channel closest to the path.

Over the centuries the river in this part of the lower Lune valley has changed course many times. Channels where the Lune once flowed have become quiet backwaters providing a natural habitat for waterfowl. In summer dense undergrowth encroaches on the path impeding progress somewhat. Small streams, forded by wooden footbridges, tumble down into the backstream.

After a short distance the path enters Wild Carr Wood. Secretive pools of backwater can occasionally be glimpsed through the dense undergrowth. A wooden footbridge is crossed before leaving the wood via a stile.

Electrified fences

The path from the Snab down to Loyn Bridge crosses the River Lune flood plain which local farmers have divided into huge grazing pastures. Electrified fences are used extensively to separate cattle and control grazing. These fences sometimes cross public rights of way and where they do so the farmer invariably provides a safe crossing point.

From the author's experience this is an area where relations between farmer and walker are good. Nevertheless, rights of way should be strictly followed and the temptation to cut corners resisted.

A wire fence bordering the path leads to a remote cottage in an area known as the Snab. Pass in front of the cottage, turn right on joining an access road, cross over a cattle-grid and walk forward a short distance to a bend in the road. At this point leave the road in favour of a track on your right. This leads down to a finger post alongside a wooden gate which admits to a very large pasture. On your right a substantial sheet of backwater is the home of two swans. The right

Fishing the Lune

As it nears the river the path swings left and for the next mile runs along the edge of a broad, flat pasture with the Lune a mere stone's throw away. Grazing cattle come close to the water's edge.

The river flowing into the Lune from the east is the Wenning which has its origins in the foothills above Ingleton. Standing on higher ground above the northern bank of the Wenning is Hornby Castle.

of way almost touches the backwater as it crosses the pasture in a south-easterly direction. The path is not well defined and a measure of luck is required to spot a wooden stile that crosses an electrified fence. Cross the stile and follow the path as it sets a course towards the Lune.

From the confluence continue along the riverside path. The large farm occupying higher ground on your left is Sandbeds and the road serving the farm is Sandbeds Lane which connects

Sandbeds Farm near Gressingham

Early spring in Gressingham

with the village of Gressingham, one mile away. Unless visiting Gressingham continue to follow the river upstream. The path enters a lovely wood via a stile. In spring clumps of wild garlic, wood sorrel, sweat violet and primroses intermingle amongst the drifts of bluebells to create a wonderful palette of colour. Leave the wood via a stile and cross the foot of a small field (a rarity in these parts!). A small gate leads into another equally delightful wood with side paths leading down to the water's edge. Exit the wood via a wooden bridge which leads into yet another large pasture. Loyn Bridge, our final objective on this section of the walk, can be seen in the distance. Cross the pasture in the direction of the bridge but keeping close to the river bank.

On the opposite bank, occupying a slightly elevated site, is Priory Farm which takes its name from

Gressingham

Gressingham is a pretty village, famed for its duck of the same name, with a lovely old church perched on a small hill with a fast flowing stream below.

To visit Gressingham leave the riverside path in favour of a tarmac lane which joins the access road to Sandbeds. Walk up the hill ignoring all side roads until the village is reached. Before making the minor detour it should be noted that Gressingham is a "dry" village and anyone seeking out a hostelry either for refreshments or to sample its native duck will be disappointed.

To rejoin the author's route follow the main road (signposted Hornby and Melling) down to Loyn Bridge. Care is required as this is a busy road with no side pavements.

Strikingly attractive houses are a feature of Gressingham

a Premonstratensian Abbey built in the 12th-century on land where the farm now stands. The Premonstratensians, who led a simple but austere life, wore a white habit and were known as the White Canons.

As you approach the bridge divert slightly to the left side where stone steps lead onto the Gressingham—Hornby road. The medieval three-arched bridge marks the end of the first section of our walk to Richmond.

To visit Hornby (half a mile via road) either take the waymarked riverside path or walk along the road — the latter being considerably shorter though less interesting.

Loyn Bridge

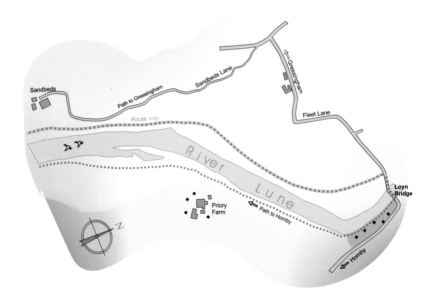

Hornby

The picturesque village of Hornby
belongs to the River Wenning, which
flows through the middle of the
village, rather than the Lune which
bypasses it by half a mile. The name
Hornby is of Scandinavian origin
but it is the Normans who left their
mark in the form of a large motte and
bailey site, Castle Stede, at the
northern end of the village above the
Lune. During the 13th-century a
new castle was built on a raised site
overlooking the River Wenning.
Little remains of the original castle
which was largely rebuilt during the
16th and 19th-centuries.

Hornby has an unusual parish
church. The octagonal tower of St
Margaret's was built in the 16th-
century to commemorate an English
victory over the Scottish army at
Flodden Field in 1513. The rest of the
church was rebuilt in 1817 and
1889.

St Margaret's Church, Hornby

Period houses, Hornby

Hornby Castle overlooking the River Wenning

Distance: 9 miles (14.5km)

Walking Time: 4 hours approximately

Terrain: Easy walking throughout the route. The section between Loyn Bridge and Melling is mainly over broad, flat and generally featureless pastures that can be quite disorientating. Navigation is further hindered by poor waymarking. Beyond Melling the terrain changes to one of undulating pastures interspersed with woodlands.

Waymarking from Melling to Ingleton is generally good.

Map: 1:25 000   OS Explorer 0L2 – Yorkshire Dales – Southern & Western Areas

Route at a Glance:

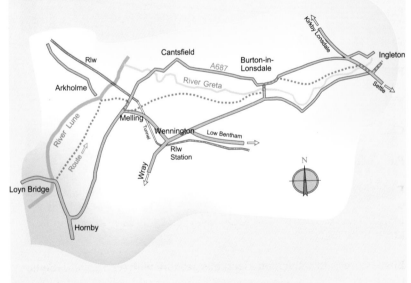

Route Overview: From Loyn Bridge the route switches to the south bank of the Lune and makes a wide sweep through the Lune flood plain towards Melling, a village situated on a broad ridge above the Lune. After Melling the route threads its way along quiet country lanes as it heads out of the Lune Valley. At the hamlet of Old Wennington the route crosses the county boundary between Lancashire and North Yorkshire as it proceeds towards Burton-in-Lonsdale, a village perched above the northern bank of the River Greta from where the route sets a course for Ingleton with the Greta in close attendance.

Accommodation: Ingleton offers a traditional Dales hotel, inns with rooms, several guest houses and B&Bs. Ingleton also has a youth hostel. The neighbouring village of Thornton-in-Lonsdale (one mile away) has a nice hotel with modern rooms.

Cafes, restaurants and tea rooms: Ingleton. Also just outside Ingleton, close to the A65/A687 junction, there is an acclaimed farmshop and cafe.

Public Houses: Ingleton, Thornton-in-Lonsdale and Burton-in-Lonsdale

Tourist Information Centre: Ingleton

Post Offices: Ingleton and Burton-in-Lonsdale

Village Shops: Ingleton and Burton-in-Lonsdale

Chemist: Ingleton

Public Toilets: Ingleton

Rail Services: Wennington (one mile from the route) with frequent direct services to Lancaster, Settle, Skipton and Leeds. The nearest railway station to Ingleton is at Bentham (four miles away) on the Leeds— Lancaster— Morecambe line.

Bus Services: Ingleton is on a local bus network with services to (1) Settle (2) Lancaster via Burton-in-Lonsdale and Bentham (3) Kendal via Kirkby Lonsdale and (4) Horton-in-Ribblesdale.

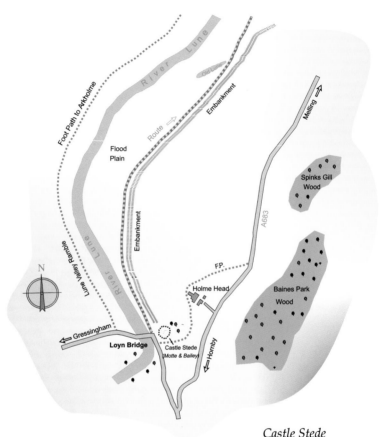

Castle Stede

From the Hornby side of Loyn Bridge proceed through a metal gate and follow a broad, stony path leading down to a large pasture above the south bank of the Lune. On your right a belt of trees forms a semi-circle round a large earthen mound known as Castle Stede.

Outside of the Welsh Borders the Lune Valley has the highest concentration of Norman castle sites in England. The defeat of King Harold at the Battle of Hastings in 1066 resulted in a change of order at the apex of English society. The vast majority of the indigenous population only became aware that a new governing class had taken over the country with the sudden appearance of huge timber towers built on raised earth and stone mounds that not only dominated the feudal landscape for miles around but also projected the military and political power of the new rulers.

Castle Stede is the largest motte and bailey site in the Lune Valley. It occupies what was once an important strategic position above the Lune. The earthworks are best viewed from a waymarked path close to a World War II pillbox located just around the corner from Loyn Bridge.

The official path, barely visible, runs alongside the foot of a flood defence embankment (left-hand side) though most walkers seem unable to resist the temptation to walk along the top of the embankment which provides a bird's eye view of the surrounding terrain.

As progress is made the sister villages of Melling, on your right, and Arkholme, straight ahead, come into sight. About a mile from Loyn Bridge the path runs alongside a watercourse at the end of which the path bears away from the embankment as it strikes a course towards Arkholme, a village lying on the opposite bank of the Lune.

Keeping the ditch, now partnered by a wire fence, on your left

A quiet backwater adopted by two swans

follow the right of way across a concrete track used by tractors. Now aim for the left-hand side of a narrow corridor of trees lying directly ahead as indicated by an easily missed waymark. As you draw level with the plantation look for a second waymark located on the upper bank of a small stream bridged by a stone slab. After crossing the stream, go through a small gate and then follow the wire fence on your left for 200 metres. Enter a long, narrow field on your left via a stile, cross the top edge and leave the field via a second stile.

Now aim for a forlorn looking plantation of deciduous trees marked on the OS map as a wood, but over the years winter storms have taken their toll turning the wood into a graveyard of broken trees. The faint path threads its way tentatively through the wind-damaged trees as it leads unerringly to the banks of the Lune. Should you lose the path merely aim for a conspicuous white house on the northern bank of the river.

On reaching the bank of the river

Melling forded the river at this idyllic spot as they went about their daily business, but for us the old ford beneath our feet represents a major turning point in our walk to Richmond. We now leave behind our silvery

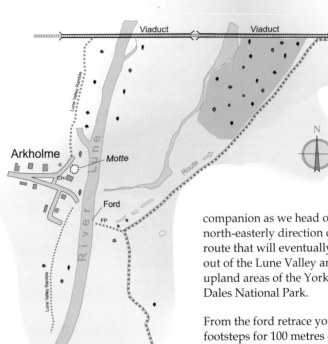

companion as we head off in a north-easterly direction on a route that will eventually take us out of the Lune Valley and into upland areas of the Yorkshire Dales National Park.

From the ford retrace your footsteps for 100 metres or so until you reach a shallow channel on your left and at the point where the path forks take the left-hand branch towards Melling. With each step the channel becomes more pronounced as it develops into open pools of water. Continue along the path

— and with the white house about 100 metres upstream — pause for a moment. Before the coming of the railway the inhabitants of Arkholme and

keeping the water channels on your left until you reach the first of two stiles close to the water's edge. After the stiles follow the path, now partnered by a hawthorn hedge on your right. Ahead is the viaduct carrying the Leeds—Lancaster—Morecambe line across the Lune Valley. On your left are the remnants of an old Lune watercourse where the river once flowed but now a veritable haven for waterfowl. As you approach the viaduct

a kissing gate located alongside a metal gate on your right admits to a green lane which runs parallel to the viaduct embankment. Pass through the kissing gate and walk forward. Melling, with its imposing stone church and large manor house, are the main focal points ahead. On reaching the A683 turn right towards the village and as quickly as possible, for it is an extremely busy road, gain the relative safety of a side

The Lune at Arkholme

St John's Church Arkholme. The Norman motte lies to the left and rear of the church.

A charming corner of Arkholme

pavement which leads to a "T" junction. At this junction cross the road and head out of the village on the much quieter Wennington road.

The fine old building on your left is Melling Hall, an 18th-century manor house and on your right, occupying a delightfully secluded position behind St Wilfrid's Church, is yet another inverted pudding basin motte.

Continue along the Wennington road as it climbs out of the

Arkholme

Arkholme can trace its history back to the Norman Conquest. The Church of St John the Baptist, built alongside a Norman motte, dates back to 1450 with a bell cote added in 1788 to house a single 14th-century bell, claimed to be one of the oldest in the country.

A public ferry, the only one on the Lune, operated downstream from the church until the 1940s.

(NB to visit Arkholme it is necessary to ford the Lune or walk along its northern bank from Loyn Bridge. Fording the river—not advisable— should only be undertaken when the river is running low and extreme care taken as the rocks below the water are slippery.)

The railway line between Leeds and Morecambe still runs through the village but the station, once one of the busiest along the line, closed in 1960.

Beautifully preserved milestones are a credit to the residents of Melling

village. Just beyond the village school a private driveway on your left leads to Galley Hill Farm and a few steps further on a quiet lane leads off from the road. Follow the lane, initially bordered by gorse and hawthorn, as it leads deeper into the Lancashire countryside with pleasant, rolling, pastures all around.

Melling Hall (centre)

The wild moors of the Bowland Forest form a wide arc across the eastern prospect and on the skyline ahead is Ingleborough, a mountain which increasingly will serve as a landmark as we approach the Yorkshire Dales National Park.

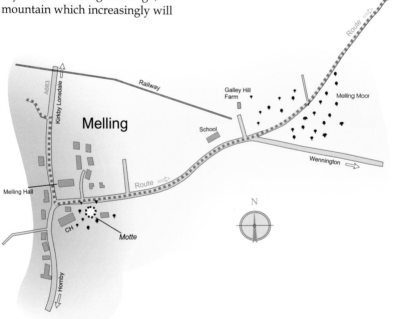

Melling

Melling lies on a broad, sunny ridge of the sweeping lower Lune Valley. It is a handsome village with fine houses dressed in mellow sandstone lining the main road. It exudes an air of prosperity, no doubt benefiting from being within easy commuting distance of Lancaster.

For all its considerable charms Melling is no longer a village at peace with itself. Tranquillity once reposed amongst its lovely old houses, back lanes and passageways. There was a time when below the weathered grave stones in the parish church burial ground the souls of the departed rested in peace. But, alas, no more. Nowadays, practically the whole village shudders and shakes as a steady stream of cavernous cattle trucks, multi-wheeled juggernauts and giant tractors, towing an array of agricultural machinery with

St. Wilfrid's Church, Melling

whirling, flashing metal blades, rattle and pound their way along the main street.

Melling can trace its history back to pre-Norman Conquest days. Inside St Wilfrid's Church, lying on a window ledge at the west end of the northern aisle, are the fragments of an Anglo Saxon preaching cross which stood originally in the grounds of the church.

In pre-Christian Britain it was Celtic custom to mark important places with rudimentary stone pillars. The early Christian missionaries adopted this practice by replacing their ornately carved wooden "rood crosses", which they carried with them as they travelled from village to village preaching the gospel, with permanent finely carved stone crosses below which the local congregation would gather. The very early churches were built on sites where the original stone preaching crosses stood.

Melling

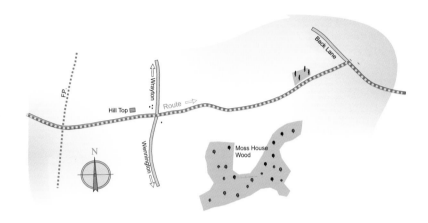

As you advance along the lane the steeple of Burton-in-Lonsdale's parish church looms into view.

After about a mile an unclassified road bisects the lane. This road connects with the villages of Wennington, less than one mile to the south, and Wrayton, three-quarters of a mile to the north-west. Continue along the lane until it terminates on meeting a second unclassified road whereupon turn right.

Immediately ahead is the charming hamlet of Old Wennington (not to be confused with the village of Wennington) which marks the terminus of our walk in Lancashire.

The boundary with North Yorkshire, the largest county in England, lies a short distance away. Yorkshire folk will no doubt quicken their pace and puff out their chests with pride as they stroll into *God's own country*. Lancastrians, on the other hand, may be forgiven if they feel a

The boundary between Lancashire and Yorkshire runs through Old Wennington

pang of sadness as they leave
behind this bewitchingly
beautiful corner of Lancashire.

The hamlet of Old Wennington

Just beyond the boundary sign
the road veers away to the right.
Leave the road as this juncture in
favour of the access road leading
to Scaleber Farm. Follow the
access road around the perimeter
of the farm and pause when you
reach a single-storey outbuilding
displaying an easily overlooked
waymark. A metal gate on your right
leads into a small paddock. Cross the
paddock and leave via a stile
which admits to a large rising
pasture. Aim half-right and walk
towards a mid-point on the rise.
(The finger on the waymark post
is accurately aligned with the
right of way.) On topping the

rise you should spot a stile
located in the south-east corner of
the pasture. Take this stile and
maintain the same line of march
as you head across the next
pasture towards the north-west
corner of Black Wood. After crossing
the next stile in the series follow the
waymarked path which runs parallel to
the northern boundary of the wood
before bearing away on a north-
easterly course as it sweeps

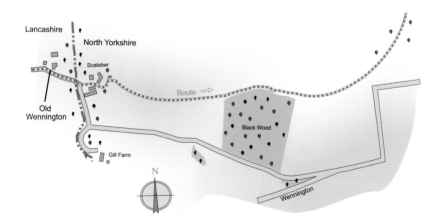

towards our next objective, Clifford Hall.

The path passes in front of Clifford Hall and to the left of a large pond. Locate a gravel path running between the main hall and a detached dwelling on the right-hand side. At first glance the gravel path has a *private, do not enter* look about it, but rest assured it is a right of way and one that leads directly onto a tarmac lane.

On joining the lane turn left and walk forward passing a farmhouse on your left. At the head of the lane take the broad track on your right leading into a delightful wood. After a short distance the track funnels into a well-trodden, single-file path that slopes down towards the River Greta. The wood contains a profusion of paths fanning out in all directions. Seek out the path that, apart from one minor deviation around the perimeter of a secluded house, tracks the Greta upstream.

Dominating the northern bank of the river is All Saints' Church whose bulky mass and towering steeple is accentuated by its

The River Greta at Burton-in-Lonsdale

hillside location. Exit the wood and follow the riverside road as far as Burton Bridge. Cross the bridge and climb the steep riverside bank into Burton-in-Lonsdale.

Burton-in-Lonsdale

Burton-in-Lonsdale lies on the steep northern banks of the River Greta. The Normans recognising its strategic importance built a castle on

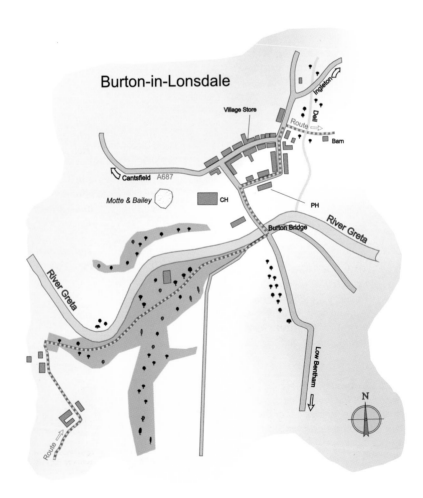

*a hillside overlooking the River
Greta. In 1274 the King granted
Burton a charter to hold a weekly
market.*

*A rectangle of four streets lined by
lovely sandstone cottages, some
dating back to the 18th century, form
the backbone of the village.*

*It is hard to imagine as you walk
these relatively quiet streets that*

Burton Bridge

The village Manor House built in 1746

*from 1740 to 1947 Burton was
engaged in no small measure in the
pottery industry. Up to 14 potteries
scattered throughout the village and
along the banks of the River Greta
produced earthenware and stoneware
vessels.*

*Virtually the whole village was
engaged in the production of pots
from digging the clay out of the local
hillside, mining coal from local
outcrops, transporting the raw
materials to the kilns for refining,
turning and firing, and delivering*

*the finished pots to market. Plumes
of dense smoke and coal dust covered
the entire village which became
known as "Black Burton".*

*The local pot making industry fell
into rapid decline as Staffordshire,
with better railway links, developed
mass production methods.*

*Today there are few signs that this
industrialisation of the village ever
took place.*

*Picturesque stone cottages overlooking an
attractive cobbled and partly paved patio,
Burton-in-Lonsdale*

All Saints' Parish Church, Burton-in-Lonsdale

Laurence Binyon

There can be few churches in England that so completely and overwhelmingly dominate their village as All Saints'. The church was consecrated in 1870 and the first vicar of Burton was Rev F Binyon, the father of Laurence Binyon (1869–1943) whose immortal poem For the Fallen *is read at Remembrance Day services throughout the Commonwealth.*

the left of the barn and maintain a beeline as you cross from one pasture to another over a series of ladder stiles, the final one being a particularly impressive structure with a platform on top.

Leave Burton on the Ingleton road. 50 metres past the housing on your right and close to a bus stop, a finger post marks a public footpath. Follow the path as it skirts around private gardens and driveways on its steep descent into a delightful dell drained by a fast flowing stream. In spring the pungent smell of wild garlic lies heavy in the dell.

Cross the stream via a wooden footbridge and climb the far bank. A stile leads into an open field with an impressive, though sadly dilapidated, barn. Pass to

Over to your right, but hidden from view, flows the River Greta. The air resounds with the constant bleating of grazing sheep. Ingleborough provides the main focus of interest ahead. On your left Barnoldswick Lane is converging on our path. Lane and pasture are separated by a wooden fence which gives way to a short section of stone walling within which there is an easily missed stile. Cross the stile, turn right and follow the lane downhill for 200 metres. On your left a signpost, located close to a stile, directs to Burton Road.

The stile leads into a pasture with a wire fence running down its eastern boundary. Cross the pasture keeping the wire fence on your right. After a short distance a stream emerges on the right-hand side of the fence. Look for a waymark in the top corner of the pasture. Proceed into and cross the next pasture maintaining the same course.

The Church of St Oswald, Thornton-in-Lonsdale, has a famous literary connection — Sir Arthur Conan Doyle, creator of Sherlock Holmes, was married in the church

In the top right-hand corner of the pasture is another stile which breaks the line of march. Enter the next pasture and make a right diagonal crossing aiming for a waymark in the far corner. Cross into the next pasture and align the line of walk with Ingleborough or in poor visibility maintain a beeline as each successive pasture is crossed until you reach Lund Farm. A large metal gate (not waymarked) provides access to

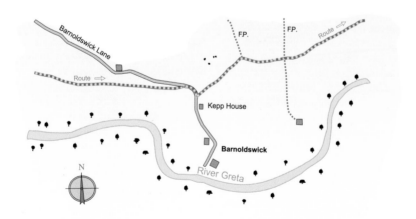

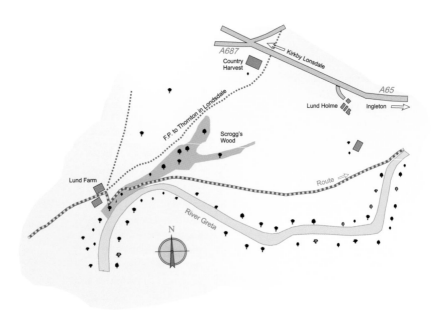

the farmyard. The right of way passes between the farmhouse, on your right, and outbuildings, on your left. Stop when you reach a second metal gate at the far end of the farmyard. Immediately beyond this gate the path forks. The higher left-hand branch shoots off in a north-easterly direction towards Thornton-in-Lonsdale passing en route Country Harvest, an acclaimed farm shop and café. The author's route, which is shorter and more attractive but not recommended after heavy rain, follows a stone wall on your right leading to a stile admitting to Scrogg's Wood. Cross the stile, turn left and follow a wire fence along the top edge of the semi-open beech wood. After a short distance the waymarked path sinks deeper into the wood. Cross a small stream running alongside a wire fence. Now cross the wire fence itself via a stile. Follow the woodland path until you come to a concrete strip bridge crossing a tributary stream of the Greta. Cross the bridge. Ahead lies a large pasture. Cross this pasture

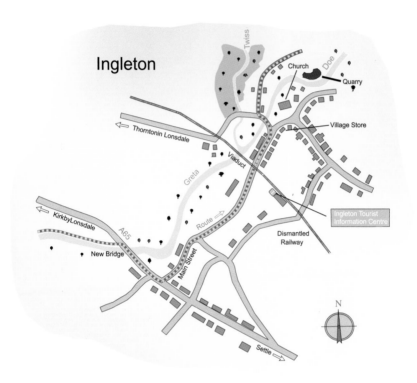

Ingleton

Twiss

Church

Doe

Quarry

Thornton in Lonsdale

Village Store

Viaduct

Greta

Ingleton Tourist
Information Centre

Kirkby Lonsdale

A65

Route

Dismantled
Railway

New Bridge

Main Street

N

Settle

aiming for a ladder stile in the far
right-hand corner close to the
river. Cross into the next pasture
but do not complete the crossing.
Instead divert to a stile which
crosses a boundary wire fence
close to the river. Follow the river
upstream until progress is
blocked by the looping Greta.
The path now enters another
pasture. Cross this pasture
keeping close to a wire fence on
your right. Leave the pasture via

a stile and follow the River Greta
upstream until you reach a small
gate. The gate leads into the final
pasture in the series. Cross the
new pasture keeping close to the
river bank. A stile and stone
steps lead onto New Bridge
which carries the A65 across the
River Greta. Cross the bridge,
walk forward to the second road
junction, turn left and follow the
main street into the village of
Ingleton.

Ingleton

Ingleton is from a geological perspective the most interesting village en route to Richmond. It lies at the foot of a glacial valley flanked by Ingleborough in the east and by the Whernside mastiff in the west. The centre of the village lies along the eastern escarpment of a steep-sided gorge scoured by the rivers Twiss and Doe. These two unusually named rivers, which merge at the viaduct to form the River Greta, create a natural phenomena of woodland glens and waterfalls that are considered the finest in England.

It is the Ingleton glens along with the spectacular caves and potholes in the surrounding hills for which Ingleton is renowned.

Ingleton's historical roots go back thousands of years. In the second millennium BC a Celtic tribe built and occupied a hill fort (the highest in the country) on the summit of Ingleborough. The remains of this Iron Age settlement are still traceable today.

The Roman infantry marched through the village on its way

The River Doe at Ingleton with charming old mill cottages abutting the river bank

No artist could fail to be inspired by Ingleton's maze of passageways lined with charming cottages

The village lies on the edge of a massive bedrock of limestone which extends deep into the Yorkshire Dales. For hundreds of years limestone has been extensively quarried, an activity which continues to this day.

The buildings of Ingleton are predominantly built of grey limestone as is Ingleton's most famous landmark, the railway viaduct which carried the now abandoned Midland Railway line high above the River Greta.

between its forts at Bainbridge and Lancaster. The Romans set up a signal station on Ingleborough using beacons of fire. In Celtic-Roman "Ingle" means fire. At the time of the Norman Conquest Ingleton was known as Inglstune, the fire town.

At one time Ingleton had a thriving coal mining industry employing up to 500 miners, but a major geological fault in the coal seam brought this

Ingleton's most famous landmark, the railway viaduct which once carried steam trains above the River Greta

activity to a premature end during
the inter-war years.

The Industrial Revolution brought
textile and tanning mills to the banks
of the rivers Twiss and Doe and
many of these long since abandoned
mills have been converted into
pleasant riverside dwellings.

Old mill cottages, Ingleton

The parish Church of St Mary stands
in a commanding position on a
plateau high above the River Doe on
a site formerly occupied by a
Norman church. The tower is
original built in the 13th-century,
but the nave is Victorian having
been rebuilt twice following
subsidence.

A quiet corner of Ingleton

St Mary's Church, Ingleton

Distance: 6½ miles (10.4 km)

Walking Time: 3½ hoursapproximately

Terrain: Strenuous walking from Ingleton to Ewes Top and easy
thereafter. The terrain is predominantly limestone with peaty sections of
moorland where the path fades. Shakeholes, potholes and deep unfenced
shafts line a substantial part of the route.

Waymarking is excellent at the beginning and at the end of the route.
However, the middle section between Scar End and Ellersbeck is poorly
waymarked.

Map: 1:25 000 OS Explorer OL2 – Yorkshire Dales – Southern & Western
Areas

Route at a Glance:

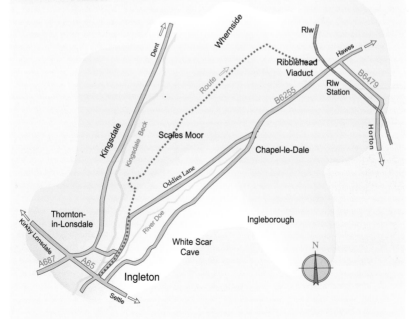

Route Overview: From Ingleton the route enters the valley of Chapel-le-Dale via a steeply rising road that runs between the rivers Twiss and Doe. It then adopts an old packhorse route making a zigzag ascent of Scar End before cutting through fragmented limestone pavements below the summit of Ewes Top. From Ewes Top the route crosses Scales Moor with its fluted potholes and erratic boulders and continues below the southern flank of Whernside passing above the farming hamlet of Chapel-le-Dale. The route then proceeds along a narrow limestone ridge passing a line of farmsteads above Winterscales Beck which is crossed before coming to rest under the arches of Ribblehead Viaduct.

Facilities: Limited unless use is made of the Settle-Carlisle Railway with southbound stops at Horton-in-Ribblesdale (5 miles away) and Settle (14 miles away). NB There are no regular bus services operating within this section of the route.

Accommodation: A roadside inn with rooms at Ribblehead. Horton-in-Ribblesdale has two traditional village hotels. Settle offers a wider range of accommodation including hotels, inns with rooms, guest houses and B&Bs.

Public Houses: Chapel-le-Dale and Ribblehead

Public Toilets: Ribblehead station (customers only)

Whernside, the highest mountain in Yorkshire, seen from limestone pastures above Chapel-le-Dale

Alternative route to Scar End

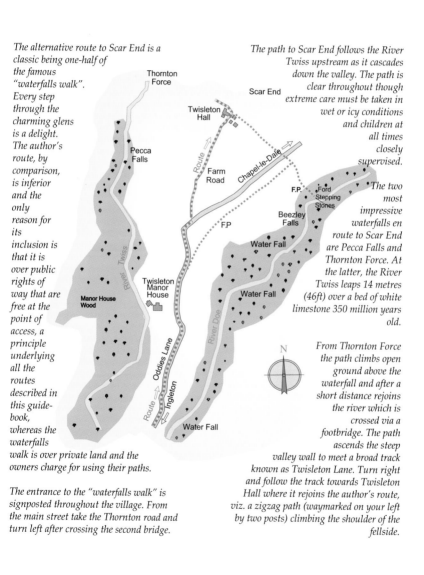

The alternative route to Scar End is a classic being one-half of the famous "waterfalls walk". Every step through the charming glens is a delight. The author's route, by comparison, is inferior and the only reason for its inclusion is that it is over public rights of way that are free at the point of access, a principle underlying all the routes described in this guide-book, whereas the waterfalls walk is over private land and the owners charge for using their paths.

The entrance to the "waterfalls walk" is signposted throughout the village. From the main street take the Thornton road and turn left after crossing the second bridge.

The path to Scar End follows the River Twiss upstream as it cascades down the valley. The path is clear throughout though extreme care must be taken in wet or icy conditions and children at all times closely supervised.

The two most impressive waterfalls en route to Scar End are Pecca Falls and Thornton Force. At the latter, the River Twiss leaps 14 metres (46ft) over a bed of white limestone 350 million years old.

From Thornton Force the path climbs open ground above the waterfall and after a short distance rejoins the river which is crossed via a footbridge. The path ascends the steep valley wall to meet a broad track known as Twisleton Lane. Turn right and follow the track towards Twisleton Hall where it rejoins the author's route, viz. a zigzag path (waymarked on your left by two posts) climbing the shoulder of the fellside.

Thornton Force

Scar End

Twisleton Hall

Pecca Falls

Route

Farm Road

Chapel-le-Dale

F.P.

Ford Stepping Stones

Beezley Falls

F.P

Water Fall

River Twiss

Twisleton Manor House

Manor House Wood

Water Fall

River Doe

Oddies Lane

N

Route

Ingleton

Water Fall

Those who have eschewed the charms of the *waterfalls walk* either on the grounds of principle or impoverishment should descend the steep road by the parish church, cross the first bridge and, before the second, turn right onto Mill Lane where there once stood a large textile mill which came to an ignominious end in 1904 following a fire. After passing modern riverside apartments the lane narrows to a single track as it begins a remorselessly steep climb out of the village. In spring the banks bordering the lane are dotted with dog roses which provide a pleasant diversion from the arduous climb. The lane (known as Oddies Lane) serves isolated farmsteads dotted along Chapel-le-Dale. It was originally a Roman road linking the Roman fort at Bainbridge in Wensleydale with the Lune Valley.

As height is gained ugly gashes and scars left behind in the surrounding hillsides by the quarrying of limestone are all too evident. On the opposite side of the valley, under the shadow of a large limestone scar, is a modest single-storey building with the word *cave* painted on its roof. This is White Scar Cave, the largest show cave in Britain.

A short distance beyond the driveway to Twisleton Manor the lane inclines to the right, and at

Pecca Falls, Ingleton Glens

the point where the lane starts to unwind pass through a metal gate on your left (not waymarked but nevertheless a right of way) onto a tarmac track leading to a working farm, which the OS map grandly denotes as Twisleton Hall, reflecting no doubt its status in former times.

Pass through the farmyard and on meeting the *waterfalls walk* track turn left passing two dwellings on your left. About 200 metres from the last building a bridleway path (waymarked by twin posts) zigzags up the shoulder of the hill. Take this path which is an ancient packhorse route, known as the Craven Old Way.

The Craven Old Way

The Craven Old Way was a high-level track between Ingleton and Dent Dale used by foot travellers and packhorse "trains". From medieval times to the coming of the turnpikes, a period of some 500 years, packhorses (20 to 40 ponies made up a typical "train") were used for transporting coal, iron ore, lead, wool and general merchandise between the Dales. The old packhorse routes can usually be identified by zigzag paths wending their way up fellsides before levelling out into a high-level causeway.

Alternative route in poor visibiliy

The route to Ribblehead via Scar End and Scales Moor should not be undertaken by inexperienced fell walkers in poor weather conditions. The path on the higher levels is faint with no waymarks; the whole area abounds with shakeholes and deep, unfenced shafts presenting a considerable hazard in mist.

Instead, continue along Oddies Lane to the village of Chapel-le-Dale. Just before the church turn left onto a tarmac road which leads to a number of outlying farmsteads. Follow the bridleway to Ellerbeck (just over a mile from the church) where the author's route can be rejoined.

Thornton Force— a site of major geological interest

Limestone pavements with Ingleborough in the background

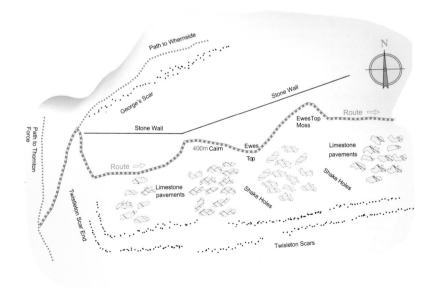

The path passes close to a small limestone outcrop before doubling back on itself. In retrospect there are superb views of the Lune Valley, the Forest of Bowland and the tidal mud flats of Morecambe Bay. Ahead, the landscape is dominated by a huge whale-back ridge leading ultimately to the summit of Whernside, which at 736 metres (2419ft) is the highest mountain in Yorkshire.

All around there are outcrops of limestone gleaming white in the sun, for this is limestone country

There are many interesting curiosities in this remarkable limestone scenery. The fluted pothole lying close to the left-hand side of the path is one such curiosity.

par excellence. The path leads round to fractured beds of limestone and a small, open shelter. Further along the path a cairn marks the summit of Ewes

The River Twiss above Thornton Force with the glaciated valley of Kingsdale beyond

Top. Where the path cuts through fractured limestone pavements it is easy to follow, but as it advances towards Scales Moor the path fades on encountering peaty sections. This is no place to wander off the path as the whole area is littered with potentially dangerous shakeholes and deep unfenced shafts. If you lose the path regain it by looking back towards Ewes Top for the alignment of the path

wall in Yorkshire, before falling away into Dent Dale, a total distance of 6 miles.

The path continues towards Scales Moor amidst remarkable limestone pavements. Along the way there are numerous erratic boulders precariously balanced on narrow stone pedestals.

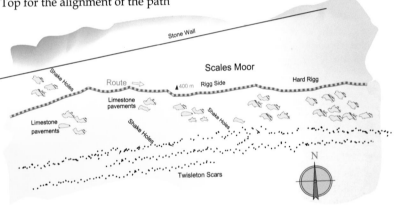

is easier to trace in retrospect than it is by looking forward!

Ignore any side branches. The path initially wanders over towards a dry stone wall on your left. Even in a county noted for its marathon running walls this wall is a true Olympian. It climbs unerringly to the summit of Whernside, making it the highest

As progress is made, the famous viaduct at Ribblehead carrying the Settle–Carlisle Railway comes into sight. Continue forward aiming for the right-hand corner of a plantation of conifer trees in the middle distance. As you approach the plantation you should spot some dilapidated railway trucks. The right of way passes to the right of these. Cross Ellerbeck Gill via the bridge and

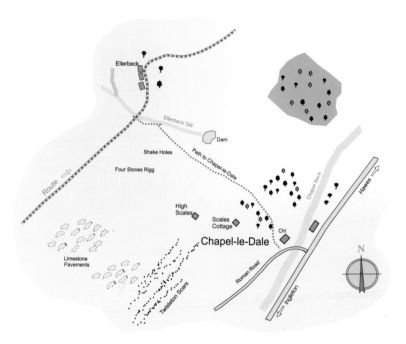

on the far side a fingerpost points towards Deepdale. This is our route but those wishing to visit the farming hamlet of Chapel-le-Dale should turn right on meeting a concrete farm track which leads directly to the settlement.

The right of way passes in front of Ellerbeck Farm which on the author's last visit was undergoing modernisation. Leave the farm via a gate and cart track. The track contours around outcrops of limestone. The views all around are of the highest order. Penyghent, which

so far has remained hidden behind Ingleborough, completes the trio of Yorkshire's iconic peaks but it is the graceful, curving viaduct at the head of Ribblesdale, our next objective, that steals the scene.

Ellerbeck Farm with its corrugated roof before modernisation

Chapel-le-Dale

The hamlet of Chapel-le-Dale is a small farming settlement grouped around the 400-year-old church of St Leonard. Inside the church is a plaque commemorating the 100 workers and their families who died either from accident or disease between 1869–1876 whilst building the Settle–Carlisle Railway. Many of the victims are buried in unmarked graves in the churchyard.

According to local legend the Romans occupied a small hillside fort above Chapel-le-Dale from which they could keep under surveillance their military road between Yorkshire and Lancashire.

An unusual sculpture in an unusual location above Chapel-le-Dale with an unusual history as recorded on a plaque at its base

St Leonard's Church, Chapel-le-Dale

The cart track leads to another secluded farm, Bruntscar. Just behind the farm, though not accessible without permission, is Bruntscar Cave which burrows deep into the hillside for half a mile.

Bruntscar lies en route to the summit of Whernside and is popular with walkers either taking part in the Three Peaks Walk or merely bagging Yorkshire's highest mountain.

At Bruntscar ignore the first finger post to Hill Inn (unless you are in urgent need of refreshment); likewise, ignore the

The Three Peaks Walk

The Three Peaks Walk is a test of physical endurance. The objective is to complete a circuit of the summit cairns of Ingleborough, Whernside and Penyghent within daylight hours. The mountains can be tackled in any order, and though there is no official route, the participants in the challenge should keep to public rights of way or access. The walk involves 1,500 metres (4,921 ft) of ascent and is approximately 25 miles long.

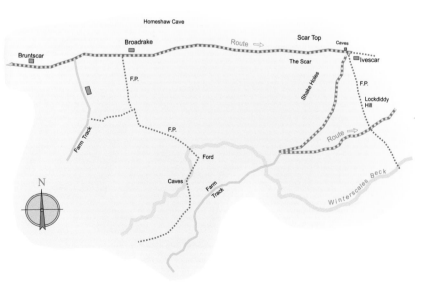

second finger post to Whernside (unless you wish to develop a rapid thirst) but seek out the third finger post, located in a corner by a small wooden gate, signed Winterscales. This is our path which crosses sloping pastures en route to the next farmstead, Broadrake.

The fields hereabouts lie on top of limestone which facilitates rapid drainage after heavy rain, thus enabling the hillside farmers to work their fields when farmers lower down the valley are mired in mud.

The right of way passes in front of the farmhouse and continues

Limestone kilns dating from about 1750 to 1860 are a common feature of the limestone Dales

across the top side of two pastures before reaching the next farmstead, Ivescar, which marks a turning point in our mid-level walk below the southern flank of Whernside. Enter the farmyard and turn right passing through a gate onto the farm access road which falls away towards Winterscales Beck in the valley below. The observant walker will

The western flank of Ingleborough, the second highest mountain in Yorkshire

notice that from Ivescar there is a
more direct path to Ribblehead
but this appears little used.
Follow the farm access road
down to Winterscales Beck and
turn left on meeting a second
farm access road which runs
alongside the beck. Follow the
track for about 200 metres before
turning right onto another track
which crosses Winterscales Beck
with Gunnerfleet Farm on your
left. This new track leads directly
to Ribblehead Viaduct.

The dark limestone arches of Ribblehead Viaduct

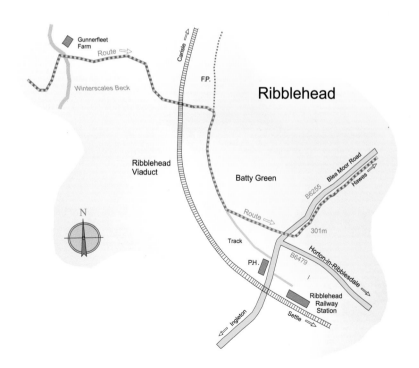

Ribblehead Viaduct

The Ribblehead Viaduct was built between 1870 and 1875 from limestone quarried locally; it is 34 metres (104ft) high and a quarter of a mile long. Not all of its 24 arches are uniform. Every sixth pier is more substantial than the rest to provide added strength to the structure.

Ribblehead station

The viaduct (originally known as Batty Moss) was built by the Midland Railway Company as part of the 72 miles long Settle–Carlisle Railway. The raison d'etre for the line was to provide a main trunk route from London to Scotland to compete with the Great Northern Railway which operated the East Coast Route via York and the North Western Railway via Crew. Until the opening of the Channel Tunnel link it was the last main trunk line to be built in England.

The construction of the railway was a major engineering achievement.

12 tunnels,15 viaducts and numerous cuttings and embankments were built to carry the line across high fells and deep valleys.

Thousands of workers, navvies, stonemasons, blacksmiths, carpenters and their wives and children lived in shanty towns close to the construction site. Over 200 workers and their families died during the construction of the railway either from accident or from an outbreak of smallpox.

Ribblehead Viaduct

Distance: 13¾ miles (22.1km)

Walking Time: 7 hours approximately

Terrain: The walk from Ribblehead to Bainbridge via Cam Fell and Wether Fell is by far the most demanding of all the routes described in this guidebook. The route is over some of the most exposed and isolated moors and fells in England and reaches 590 metres (1935ft) at its highest point and for 10 miles sustains a height above 305 metres (1000ft). It should not be undertaken by inexperienced fell walkers in winter, early spring or late autumn. Even in summer the weather can change suddenly and all walkers should be properly equipped for high-level fell walking.

Maps: (1) 1:25 000 OS Explorer OL2 – Yorkshire Dales – Southern & Western Areas and (2) 1:25 000 OS Explorer OL30 – Yorkshire Dales – Northern & Central Areas

Route at a Glance:

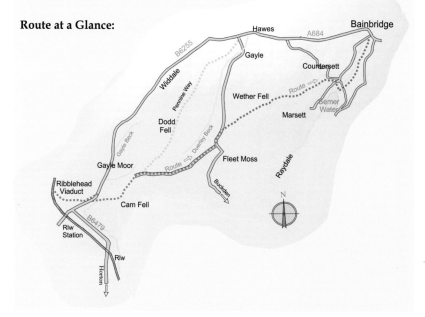

Route Overview: From Ribblehead Viaduct the route briefly joins the Ingleton–Hawes road which it leaves at Far Gearstones in favour of a steeply rising track to Cam End from where it follows a moorland ridge across Cam Fell towards Cam Houses. Beyond Cam Houses and without any significant rise or fall in gradient the route contours around the southern slopes of Dodd Fell Hill crossing the Pennine watershed at Cold Keld Gate. After Cold Keld Gate the route drifts towards the northern rim of the Wharfe Valley and at Green Side End joins Fleet Moss Pass, a high-level, unclassified motor road linking Wensleydale and Wharfedale. The route briefly follows the road towards Hawes before joining a bridleway passing below the summit of Wether Fell. On a declining gradient path the route enters Raydale passing high above the farming outpost of Marsett and the Ice Age lake of Semer Water. The route leaves the fells behind at Crag Side Road which it follows to Semer Water Bridge via Countersett. From Semer Water Bridge the route follows the River Bain downstream and enters Bainbridge via Bracken Hill.

Accommodation: Bainbridge has a village inn with rooms and a deluxe country house hotel overlooking the River Ure as well as B&Bs in season. Askrigg (one mile away) has a hotel, several guest houses and B&Bs. Hawes (four miles away) offers a wider range of accommodation including a traditional market-town hotel, several inns with rooms, guest houses and B&Bs. Remote Cam Houses, close to the route, has a dinner, B&B farmhouse. Hawes has a youth hostel.

Cafes, restaurants and tea rooms: Bainbridge, Askrigg and Hawes

Public Houses: Bainbridge, Askrigg and Hawes

Post Offices: Askrigg and Hawes

Village Shops: Bainbridge, Askrigg and Hawes

Chemist: Hawes

Public Toilets: Askrigg and Hawes

Rail Services: The nearest railway station to Bainbridge is 10 miles away at Garsdale on the Settle–Carlisle main line.

Bus Services: Regular local bus services operate between Hawes, Bainbridge, Askrigg, Leyburn, Bedale and Northallerton.

From the viaduct follow the surfaced track towards the Ingleton–Hawes road passing the site of the Ribblehead railway construction camp where 2000 workers, navvies, stonemasons, blacksmiths, carpenters and their families were housed. The site is now a Scheduled Ancient Monument. After a short distance a rightward slanting path on

A well-maintained milestone alongside the old Lancaster to Richmond turnpike

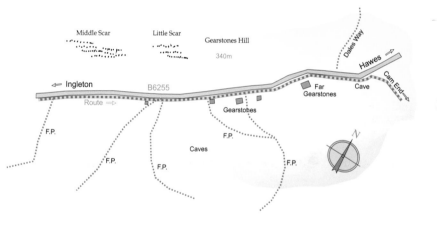

your left provides a short cut to a higher point on the unfenced B6255. On meeting the road turn left and walk forward for one mile along the wide, grass verge which in summer resembles a car park as visitors to the area break their journey to photograph the iconic viaduct or wander

Gayle Moor and Beck from Far Gearstones

amongst its dark, limestone
arches.

Gearstones Lodge (an outdoor
activities centre) on your right is
a former coaching inn which
stood alongside the Lancaster-
Richmond turnpike. In the 18th-
and 19th-centuries Gearstones
held regular fairs where Scottish
drovers would sell their High
and Lowland cattle to English
buyers. The practice of driving
cattle from Scotland to northern
England via the dales using a
network of drove roads died out
with the coming of the railways.

150 metres from Gearstones
Lodge, at the point where the
road inclines leftwards, a broad,
stony track on your right leads
down to a ladder stile adjacent to
a wooden gate and a finger post
signed Cam End. For the next

2 ¼ miles our route coincides
with the Dales Way, a long-
distance trail from Ilkley in West
Yorkshire to the shores of
Windermere in Cumbria. Cross
the stile and follow the track
down to Gayle Beck, a major
tributary of the River Ribble. A
footbridge built on substantial

stone pillars alongside an old ford provides a dry crossing of the beck.

Now take a deep breath and prepare for a hard slog up an interminably long, steeply rising rough track towards Cam End. As height is gained vast swathes of wild, wind-swept, unbroken moorland unfold beneath a huge sky. In early summer lapwings with their striking black and white plumage hover over head before breaking into violent wing-flapping, zigzagging decoy runs.

At Cam End our route is joined by another long-distance trail, the Pennine Way coming up from Horton-in-Ribblesdale. From the signpost the deeply rutted track rises steadily for the next mile as

Gayle Beck, a major tributary of the River Ribble

The Devil's Causeway

The route from Far Gearstones to Bainbridge via Cam End and Wether Fell largely follows the line of a well-engineered military road built by the Romans linking their forts at Ribchester and Lancaster with Bainbridge in Wensleydale.

In the 1750's the Roman road was improved and resurfaced and incorporated into a new turnpike road linking Lancaster and Richmond. However, sections of the route proved to be too steep for the horse-pulled wagons and carts and in 1795 the turnpike was rerouted through Hawes and Widdale.

Over the centuries the high level route linking Lancashire with Yorkshire has borne several names including The Devil's Causeway, Cam High Road (its official OS name) or simply Roman Road. But the more evocative Devil's Causeway is perhaps a more fitting name for such a lonely and bleak stretch of highway.

it follows a moorland ridge towards a waymarked cairn from where the Dales Way peels off to follow a lower course en route to the Oughtershaw Valley in Upper Wharfedale. From the cairn take the higher track which continues to follow the moorland ridge. The views down into the valley below are spoilt by over extensive forest plantations that sweep up the fellside like an incoming tide. The isolated farmhouse coming into view beyond the conifer plantation is

A moorland signpost half-buried with stones donated by walkers

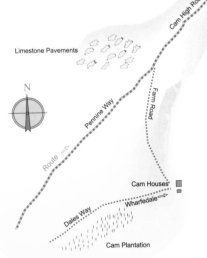

Camm Farm, also known as Cam Houses, the site of an ancient farming settlement. The farm access road joins our route below an outcrop of limestone pavements largely hidden behind a narrow scar. For the next 3 miles the track is surfaced as it contours around the lower southern slopes of Dodd Fell with hardly any rise or fall in gradient, a remarkable testament to the skills of the Roman engineers.

Less than half a mile along the disintegrating tarmac road is a fairly ordinary looking gate enclosed on either side by limestone walls. This is Cold Keld Gate (Gate is derived from the old Norse word Gata meaning street or road) and marks the boundary between the District of Craven and the District of Richmondshire but perhaps more interestingly the stone walling follows the Pennine watershed. From here to Richmond all water courses drain not into the Irish Sea, as hitherto, but into the North Sea.

300 metres beyond Cold Keld Gate we encounter another barrier in the form of Kid How Gate, which is an important junction for walkers for at this spot the Pennine Way bears away northwards on a course that takes it into Upper Wensleydale via an old packhorse route known as West Cam Road. Our route

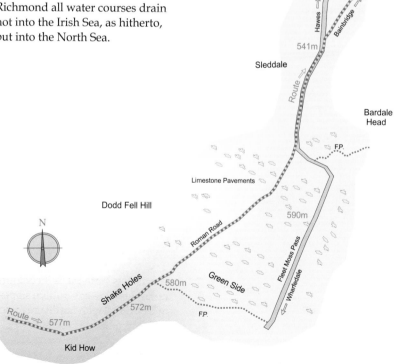

Hawes

Bainbridge

541m

Sleddale

Route

Bardale Head

F.P.

Limestone Pavements

Dodd Fell Hill

590m

N

Roman Road

Fleet Moss Pass

Shake Holes

Green Side

Wharfedale

580m

572m

F.P.

Route ⇒ 577m

Kid How

continues to follow the course of the Roman Road.

From the finger post head towards a metal gate some 30 metres away. Beyond the gate the road briefly flirts with the northern rim of the Wharfe valley basin where the River Wharfe is being born from the numerous becks and rills cascading down the steep valley walls.

After passing between a line of shakeholes on your left and an outcrop of fractured limestone pavements on your right, the road eventually reaches yet another metal gate, the final one in the series before joining Fleet Moss Pass, a high-level, unclassified motor road linking Wensleydale and Wharfedale.

At the junction turn left and follow the road for half a mile. On your right, at the point where the road begins a very steep descent, the old Roman Road is rekindled in the form of a broad

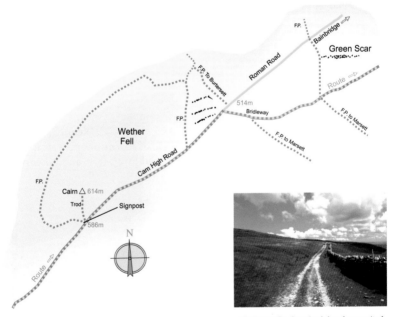

The Roman Road passing below the summit of Wether Fell

bridleway track striking out towards Wether Fell.

Before leaving Fleet Moss Pass take stock of the situation. By the most direct route Bainbridge is almost 6 miles away. In severe weather or failing daylight the road to Hawes (3 miles away) offers an escape route.

Leave the road and proceed along the bridleway as it climbs steadily towards Wether Fell. The views all around are spectacular. On your left the valley of Sleddale nestles in the lee of Dodd Fell Hill and on your right, in stark contrast to the green hues of Sleddale, is Bardale Head, barren, austere, gloomy even in bright sunlight.

Ahead and slightly to the right lies Wether Fell, the most accessible mountain in Wensleydale and a popular venue for hang-gliders and paragliders. The bridleway runs just below the summit which bears the curious name of Drumaldrace on the OS map. At 590 metres (1935ft) above sea level our walk to Richmond has attained its highest elevation, and so too has the Roman Road.

On a slowly declining gradient the Roman Road makes a rare

A paraglider prepares to take off on Wether Fell

departure from its customary Roman straightness by contouring around the head of a gill.

Continue along the Roman Road until you reach a signpost on your right-hand side for Crag Side Road and, unless taking the alternative route (described on page 87), leave the Roman Road for the signed bridleway. After passing through a metal gate walk alongside a deeply rutted track of hideous appearance created by tractors and other off-

An untidy and insignicant cairn marks the top of Wether Fell

Wether Fell Summit

Whilst there are no official rights of way over the summit plateau, walkers usually find their way to the summit cairn, located on the south-west tip of Wether Fell, via a slanting trod which joins the Roman Road close to a bridleway signpost located where the road is not fully enclosed by walls.

The extra effort is rewarded with splendid panoramic views of Upper Wensleydale. Across the valley floor are a range of ridges all above 610 metres (2000ft). Opposite is Great Shunner Fell, which carries the Pennine Way on its route into Durham. Great Shunner Fell is flanked on the left by High Seat, Wild Boar Fell and Baugh Fell, and on the right by Lovely Seat which separates Wensleydale from Swaledale. Looking westwards are two familiar friends, Whernside and Ingleborough. In the south-west Penyghent is prominent and in the south-east so too is Buckden Pike, Wharfedale's second highest mountain.

The urge to explore the summit plateau should be resisted as it is covered in unpleasant and potentially dangerous peat hags.

Cragdale, a subsidiary dale of Raydale, is classic Dales' landscape at its finest

road vehicles before the introduction of the environmentally less damaging quad bikes that today are widely used by hill farmers. These ubiquitous machines with their plump tyres and, invariably, with a sheepdog crouched over the rear axle skim across the upland terrain without recourse to cart tracks, lanes, roads and the like.

After a short distance pass through a wooden gate and continue along the falling-gradient track until you reach a crossroads of paths. The path crossing our route in a north–south orientation leads to the farming settlement of Marsett and, unless visiting Marsett, in which case turn right and follow the path down the steep fellside, continue along the bridleway which affords splendid views of Raydale and its two subsidiary dales, Bardale, virtually treeless, and Cragdale with its conifer plantations. Overhead a curlew circles.

The gated path passes through rough fellside pastures where the farmers of Raydale have grazed their cattle since time immemorial.

Further on the path passes below a line of shattered crags.

Alternative route to Bainbridge

The alternative route to Bainbridge is slightly shorter than the author's and even in heavy mist is easy to follow. However, apart from the first half mile, scenically it is less interesting with the flat ridge of Crag obscuring the finest views of Raydale and Semer Water.

The Roman Road above Bainbridge High Pasture has been worn down to its bedrock

Instead of taking the bridleway to Crag Side Road continue along the Roman Road, which in places has been worn down to its bedrock —perhaps not surprising after 2000 years of use—as it gradually loses elevation on its long, tedious, stony descent towards Bainbridge. After 1 ½ miles the Roman Road is crossed by an unclassified road linking Countersett in Raydale with Burtersett in Wensleydale. Ignore this road. Continue forward as the Roman Road resumes its straight—as—an—arrow descent into Bainbridge High Pasture eventually terminating on joining the Countersett road above Bainbridge. From here it is an easy stroll down to the village.

Marsett and Countersett

Marsett and Countersett are ancient farming communities founded by Scandinavian settlors a 1,000 years ago. The suffix "sett" derives from the Norse word "saetr" meaning a temporary dwelling on land used for hill grazing during the summer.

Marsett today is truly Orwellian: farm animals have taken over the entire settlement and their rule is absolute. Cattle are everywhere; their command centre is the village green from where they launch frequent forays along the back lanes leading to the hillside pastures; they can be seen patrolling the passageways between the lovely old rustic buildings; and they are well-

A pair of stone cottages sheltering in a fold in the hills below Crag

practised in the art of deception, appearing and disappearing in the blink of an eye.

Countersett is a charming hamlet situated in a secluded fold in the hills below Crag. The houses date from the mid-17th-century and look as if they have been randomly dropped from the sky. Quakerism was the

There is an agelessness about Marsett that is rarely found even in the remotest villages of the Dales

dominant religion of Raydale before Methodism swept through the dale. Countersett Hall was the home of Richard Robinson, the first Quaker in Wensleydale, and for many years was used as a meeting house. In 1677 George Fox stayed a night in the Hall.

Countersett Hall

The views from this section of the bridleway are the loveliest of all. In the valley bottom lies Semer Water, a jewel of a lake encompassed by a magnificent bowl of hills. Ahead lies Addlebrough on whose higher slopes Iron Age people once lived in their little round huts.

On reaching Crag Side Road turn right and walk down the hill to the crossroads. Our next

The northern tip of Semer Water with Addlebrough recognisable by its plateau top rising above Raydale

objective, Semer Water Bridge, lies at the bottom of the steep hill. To visit Countersett, a mere stone's throw away, turn left at the crossroads.

At the foot of the hill cross Semer Water Bridge, take the stile on your left (signposted Bainbridge) and follow the riverside path across three meadows to a footbridge which crosses a minor tributary of the reedy Bain,

Semer Water

Semer Water is a natural lake formed during the last Ice Age. Retreating ice left a pile of debris (a moraine) at the foot of the valley which acted as a Dam. The lake covers an area of 26.3 hectacres (65 acres), greater after heavy rain, and has a maximum depth of l0.6 metres (35ft). At one time the lake was considerably larger but draining for land reclamation in the 1930s almost halved its surface area.

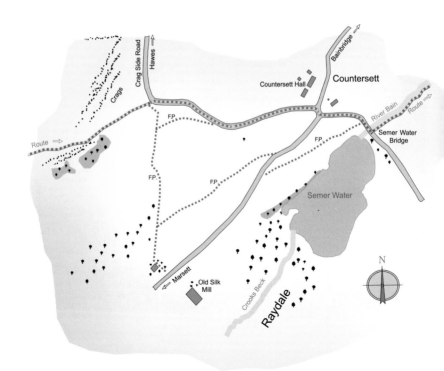

*The lowering of the water level
revealed a Bronze Age Village.*

*The Carlow Stone at the foot of Semer Water is
a classic example of an erratic boulder deposited
by melting ice 11,000 years ago*

banked by gently slopping
meadows, which meanders
sedately down Raydale. The
River Bain is reputed to be the
shortest river in England bearing
a name. After the footbridge the
path sets a beeline for Bracken
Hill. The river disappears from
view as it veers away from the

line of walk before plunging into
a thickly wooded gorge. Three
gap stiles lead to the summit of

*Surprisingly there are few natural lakes within the Yorkshire Dales National Park. Semer Water is stunningly attractive off-
setting a numerical deficit with sublime beauty*

Bracken Hill which, though of modest height, provides splendid panoramic views of neighbouring hills and valleys.

Looking backwards Semer Water looks serenely beautiful set against a backdrop of magnificent hills. Ahead the Ure valley sweeps gracefully below the scars of Whitfield and Ellerkin. From the summit cross a stile and follow a well-defined, green track as it descends the hillside. At the foot of the hill the Bain has been rejuvenated

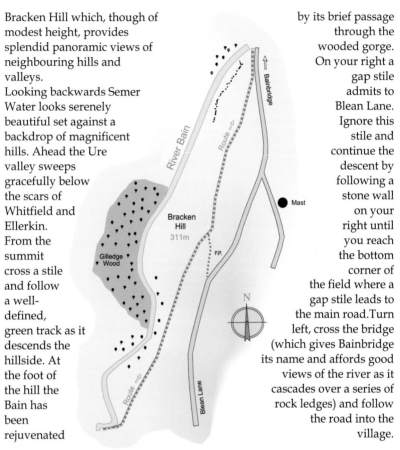

by its brief passage through the wooded gorge. On your right a gap stile admits to Blean Lane. Ignore this stile and continue the descent by following a stone wall on your right until you reach the bottom corner of the field where a gap stile leads to the main road. Turn left, cross the bridge (which gives Bainbridge its name and affords good views of the river as it cascades over a series of rock ledges) and follow the road into the village.

Semer Water Bridge

The reedy Bain

The River Bain and the village of Bainbridge seen from Bracken Hill. The Roman Fort of Virosidum occupied the higher ground above the dwellings on the far right

Bainbridge

Bainbridge comprises clusters of attractive hamlets linked together by one of the finest village greens in the north of England. The village lies on the west bank of the River Bain above the confluence with the Ure; it straddles the main road between Northallerton and Hawes. In most Dales villages the parish church is the main focal point. Bainbridge is unusual in that it has no church. Its place is taken by a highly conspicuous white-washed, 15th-century inn situated at the head of the green. No church could occupy a finer position.

The Romans recognised the strategic importance of the Bainbridge site, which lies close to the epicentre of the Dales and which became an important crossroads on their network of roads. On the directions of Julies Agricola the Roman Legions built a wooden fort on a drumlin (Brough Hill) on the eastern side of the village above the Bain. For nearly 300 years between AD95 and AD 395 soldiers numbering up to 500 were garrisoned at Virosidum, as the fort was called, to protect the region against incursions and uprisings by the restless Celtic tribes of Yorkshire.

The River Bain at Bainbridge

The white-washed "Rose and Crown" dating from the 15th century and guardian of the Forest Horn

After the Norman Conquest Bainbridge became the headquarters of 12 forest wardens whose duty was to police the ancient Forest of Wensleydale and preserve the hunting rights (mainly deer and wild boar) for the King and his lords.

During the medieval period dangers lurked in the Forest where bears and wolves roamed and guides were engaged to show travellers the way.

It became custom for a bullock horn to be blown every evening in Bainbridge to guide those still in the Forest to the safety of the village before nightfall. This custom continued down the centuries until relatively recently but sadly the old Forest Horn is now silent.

An old corn mill built about 1770 alongside the River Bain

A secluded cottage, Bainbridge

Distance: 7½ miles (12.2km)

Walking Time: 4 hours approximately

Terrain: Easy to moderate walking throughout the route through meadows and grazing pastures, along riverside paths and fellside terraces. The route throughout is exceptionally well waymarked.

Map: 1:25 000 OS Explorer OL30 — Yorkshire Dales — Northern & Central Areas

Route at a Glance:

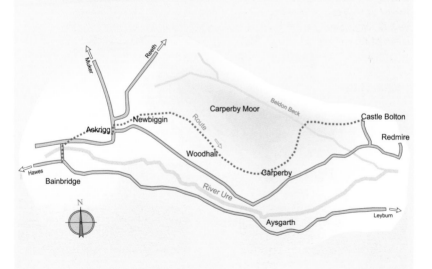

Route Overview: From Bainbridge the route follows the Askrigg Road to Yorebridge and after crossing the River Ure it proceeds on a north-easterly course towards Mill Gill where it crosses Mill Gill Beck before entering Askrigg via a stone causeway. From Askrigg the route ascends hillside pastures before entering Newbiggin, a tiny settlement nestling under the lee of Ellerkin Scar. From Newbiggin the route follows an ancient packhorse route along a narrow fellside terrace passing old lead workings and prehistoric settlements above the hamlets of Nappa Scar and Woodhall. After passing above the village of Carperby the route changes course seeking out higher ground below Locker Tarn before realigning itself with Bolton Castle. The route enters the village of Castle Bolton via the north—west tower of the castle.

Accommodation: Carperby has an interesting residential hotel with a *Herriot* connection and the neighbouring village of Aysgarth (famous for its falls) offers a residential hotel, a village inn with rooms and several B&Bs. Redmire (less than a mile from Castle Bolton) has a traditional inn with B&B.

Cafes, restaurants and tea shops: Castle Bolton (inside Bolton Castle)

Public Houses: Carperby, Redmire and Aysgarth

National Park Information Centre: Aysgarth

Public Toilets: Castle Bolton

Rail Services: The nearest main line stations to Castle Bolton are (1) Garsdale (19 ½ miles away) on the Settle—Carlisle line and (2) Northallerton (23 ½ miles away) on the East Coast Line.

Bus Services: A regular service operates between Northalleton and Hawes via Castle Bolton and Carperby.

Leave Bainbridge on the Askrigg road passing to the right of the Rose and Crown Hotel and to the left of the Friends' Meeting House. Continue down the hill to Yore Bridge passing on your right Yore Bridge House (now an attractive country house hotel) formerly the Bainbridge Grammar School founded in 1601 and closed in 1931 on moving to Askrigg. Cross the River Ure which until the 18th century was also known as the Yore. Indeed

Yoredale is the ancient name of Wensleydale which is unique amongst the principal Yorkshire Dales in that it is the only dale named after a village (Wensley), and not its river.

Now take the first stile on your right and make a left diagonal crossing of the riverside field. The flagstoned path leads to a concrete strip bridge accessed by a wicket gate. Do not cross the bridge but turn left and pass

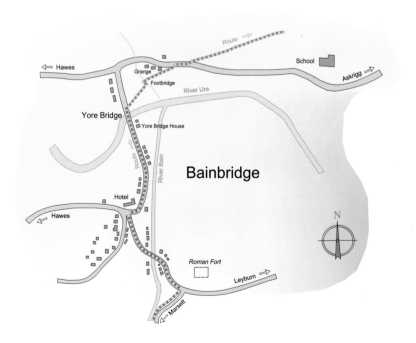

beneath a redundant railway bridge (the line, which originally ran between Northallerton on the East Coast Main Line and Garsdale on the Settle—Carlisle line, was closed to passengers in 1954) and head towards a stone footbridge with iron railings mounted on the parapets. The tiny bridge is a joy to behold. Its history is unknown but it may have been built by the monks of Jervaulx Abbey. Cross the bridge and proceed through two wicket gates bordering a farm track, the second of which leads into a paddock belonging to Grange Farm. Leave the paddock via a stile and follow a single-file path

Fors Abbey

Grange Farm occupies the site of Fors Abbey which was founded by a small group of Cistercian monks in 1145 but abandoned after a desperate struggle against the forces of nature. The weather was harsh, crops failed and wolves were a constant threat. And if that was not enough to contend with the Black Death arrived in 1148.

For 11 years the dedicated brotherhood battled against the elements and the plague before giving up the unequal struggle.

The monks retreated to East Witton,

This exquisite medieval single-arched bridge topped with iron railings was probably built as a footbridge, it being far too narrow to have served as a packhorse bridge.

across two pastures to a gap stile in a stone wall admitting to the main road. Turn right and take the first stile on your left and make a right diagonal crossing of six fields. On reaching Mill Gill take the footbridge across Mill Beck and, unless visiting Mill Gill Force (recommended), follow the downstream path which, for all too brief a period, runs alongside the beck with its lovely pools of shaded water before bearing away towards an old corn mill. This is one of three mills which

a less exposed site lower down the valley, from where Jervaulx Abbey came into existence.

A grange and chantry chapel were maintained at Fors until the Dissolution.

in former times drew water from Mill Beck for their power. The water from the beck has also been used to generate electricity for Askrigg which was of the first

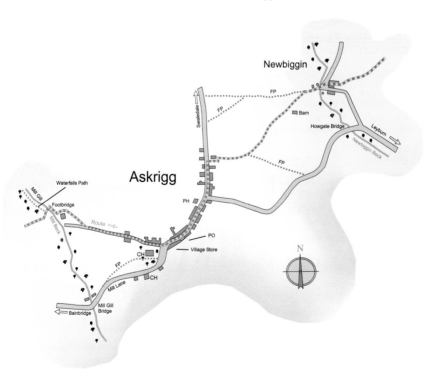

Mill Gill Force

*Whitfield Gill
and
The Waterfalls of Mill Gill*

Both Wordsworth and Turner were captivated by the waterfalls of Mill Gill and Whitfield Gill. Mill Gill is the more impressive of the two and is 600 metres upstream from the little footbridge which crosses Mill Beck.

The walk to Mill Gill Force, especially in late autumn when the leaves of the beech trees are turning colour, is a memorable experience. NB The banks of Mill Gill are quite steep in places and children should be closely supervised.

villages in England to be lit by electricity.

A flagstoned path circumvents the former mill and crosses a field on the outskirts of the village. Askrigg is noted for its flagstoned paths (locally known as causeys) which fan out in all directions from the village. Causeys were built in the 18th century to provide a dry route between Askrigg and neighbouring villages and mills. The path leads onto Mill Lane. Turn left and follow the lane to St Oswald's Church and thence into the cobbled market place with its

A flagstoned path or "causey" leading to a former corn mill in Askrigg. The word "causey" is Norman French in origin.

stepped Victorian market cross.

Next to the cross, set into the cobbles, is an ancient stone and iron ring used to tether bulls for the cruel sport of baiting. A few metres away from the cross stands an interesting, cylindrical stone pump.

A characterful sign made from an old mill stone

Askrigg

Askrigg lies on the northern side of Wensleydale between the River Ure and Ellerkin Scar. The main street is lined with 18th-and early-19th-century three-storey town houses which would not look out of place in York or Bristol. Behind these handsome Georgian houses are half-secreted passageways leading to rustic cottages huddled together in small courtyards. Standing in the midst of the village overlooking a small cobbled market place is a

St Oswald's Church, Askrigg, is a Grade I listed building

remarkable 15th-century church with a substantial tower, a broad nave and a fine leaded roof.

Askrigg first came to prominence during the reign of Elizabeth I who granted a market charter in 1587.

For almost two centuries Askrigg was the dominant settlement in upper Wensleydale. The coast to coast road from Darlington to Lancaster ran through the town bringing much business to its market. The town became prosperous.

The main street Askrigg lined with Georgian houses

At this time Hawes, its close neighbour, was a quiet backwater. But the situation was reversed after 1795 when a new turnpike road to Lancaster via Hawes was built on the south side of the River Ure. Askrigg lost its market to Hawes which rapidly developed into the main market town of Upper Wensleydale.

The stepped Victorian market cross with a famous television film set house opposite

During the 18th and 19th-centuries Askrigg was renowned for its

A delightful row of former mill workers' cottages, Askrigg

A charming old passageway in Askrigg

clockmaking. Askrigg clocks were sold throughout the northern Dales. A long case clock was frequently the first item of furniture acquired by newlyweds.

More recently Askrigg has acquired a certain celebrity status as a film set. Devotees of the BBC television series All Creatures Great and Small *will instantly recognise the handsome three-storey Georgian House opposite the market cross as Skeldale house in the series.*

From the market cross head up the main street passing on your left the King's Arms which started life as racing stables in 1750 (circa) and converted to an inn around 1800. During the filming of *All Creatures Great and Small* the inn was fictionally reincarnated as *The Drovers Arms.*

Walk forward passing on your left the Crown Inn (no reincarnation for this unpretentious village local) and at the road junction bear left (signposted Muker).

Less than 200 metres along the steeply rising road a triangular green on your right is partially enclosed by two charming cottages lying at right angles to each other with a right of way

The rooftops of Askrigg with Crag prominent on the skyline (far right)

The emblematic Swaledale breed of sheep

A well-maintained stone barn on the edge of Newbiggin

running between them. Pass in front of the cottage with the splendid wrought iron gate inset with the letters *EP* and pause when you reach the garage. To the right of the garage a half-hidden stile leads into a hillside pasture. Take the stile and follow a well-defined, single-file path that climbs the hillside pasture in a north-easterly direction. Continue on the same course through a series of pastures and stiles passing to the left of an isolated field barn. As height is gained the views across the Ure valley are exquisite. Beyond Bainbridge the Roman Road can be seen striking out for the summit of Wether Fell. On the opposite side of the valley Addlebrough, resembling an upturned boat, presents its most interesting flank. Snuggling between these two icons of Upper Wensleydale is the cool, green valley of Raydale. Ahead

lies the hamlet of Newbiggin, our next objective, nestling below the broad flank of Ellerkin Scar.

From the isolated barn the path falls away towards a stone wall where it terminates alongside a wooden gate. Pass through the gate and turn right along a walled lane leading to a stone bridge crossing a fast flowing beck. Cross the bridge and enter Newbiggin. (The name has Norse origins and means new buildings.)

Nappa Hall, a rare, for the Dales, fortified manor house of the mid-15th century

Downtown Newbiggin!

The tiny settlement of Newbiggin nestling under Ellerkin Scar

Keeping the small green and tree on your right, pass in front of a row of lovely sandstone cottages. After the last cottage on your left go through a metal gate and take a half-left, aiming for a gap stile on the far side of the pasture. The path now runs parallel to a wall for about 100 metres. Proceed through a gap stile on your left and make a right diagonal crossing of the pasture, aiming for a small wood below the lower slopes of Ellerkin Scar.

The path passes the top left-hand corner of a large barn (incidentally, the OS 1:25 000 map shows the right of way passing the lower right-hand corner!) before swinging round to the right as it closes in on the wood. Follow the broad, green path as it climbs gently through the delightful semi-open wood.

On the far side of the wood proceed through two gap stiles appearing in quick succession and continue to follow the path as it resumes its rightward diagonal climb across open fields towards an enclosed lane. Join the lane through a squeeze-through stile and turn right. The lane is in places deeply rutted and following rain invariably muddy. After 100 metres the lane bifurcates with one branch peeling off to the right (this branch leads to the hamlet of Nappa Scar and Nappa Hall) and

Ellerkin Scar rising above Newiggin

the other branch bearing away leftwards towards higher ground above a farmhouse. Follow the higher track (signposted Castle Bolton). Pass through a gate adjacent to a barn on your right. Shortly, the wall on your left gives way to a line of shakeholes with vast tracts of rough, open moorland beyond. The wall on your right continues for a while

Oxclose Road after rain

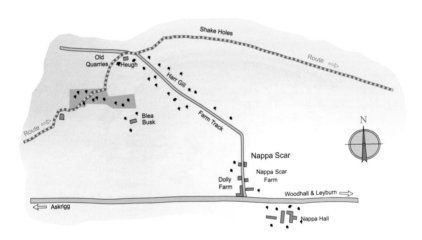

longer until this too runs its course. The views the length and breadth of Wensleydale are breathtaking. Ahead, forming a barrier across the lower dale is the shapely profile of Penhill, Wensleydale's most recognisable landmark. Pass through a second gate. The wall, temporarily reinstated on your right, drifts

away southwards. Pass through another gate and immediately the broad, green track with its fine springy turf takes on the appearance of a fairway. On your right a corridor of trees runs parallel to the fairway. At the end of the fairway there are huge bunkers which are, in fact, old lead mines. In the early days of lead mining rudimentary bell-shaped pits were sunk by miners at regular intervals along a vein of lead and waste material from the mine dumped around the perimeter of the pit.

Now pass through a further gate to the right of which stands a finger post and follow the broad track downhill for about 75 metres. On your left, with the rooftops of Woodhall a mere stone's throw away, a second finger post adjacent to a small gate directs to Carperby and

A view from Heugh looking towards the hamlet of Nappa Scar

Old bell-shaped lead mines above Woodhall

The path to Castle Bolton crosses the head of several small gills

Castle Bolton. Proceed through the gate and follow the uphill path which swings rightwards to join a broad, green track known as Oxclose Road.

Oxclose Road, now a bridleway, was once a medieval packhorse route between Askrigg and Castle Bolton. After a short distance the bridleway is bisected by a stream. Ford the stream above a waterfall known as Disher Force. Care should be exercised in crossing the stream particularly after heavy rain, and children should not be allowed to venture near the waterfall which crashes down a precipitous and dangerous gill.

Above the ford are the remains of a prehistoric settlement.

Proceed through a gate on the far side of the stream and continue

Penhill

Penhill is the best known of the Wensleydale Fells. It forms a massive bulkhead between Waldendale and Coverdale. Its impressive northern flank creeps down into Wensleydale forming a barrier above West Witton. Penhill can be seen from as far a way as the North Yorkshire Moors. Indeed such is its prominence that during the Napoleonic Wars, and possibly long before, its domed summit formed a chain of country-wide beacons which were lit at times of impending national danger.

Penhill, Wensleydale's most recognisable mountain

along the bridleway which passes to the south of old, lead mine workings below Ivy Scar. The track is easy to follow being lined with long furrows created by farm vehicles. The track gently rises towards a prominent gap in a stone wall which can be seen in the middle distance.

As progress is made a radio mast located on Carperby Moor, higher up the fellside, comes into view. The track reaches a metal gate (Oxclose Gate). On the far side of the gate the path forks. Our route continues in a straight line across the pasture and through the gateless opening in the stonewall. The broad, green path crosses several more pastures before reaching a farm lane (Peatmore Lane). Cross the lane and take a stile into a large pasture. The path gradually drifts away from the wall on your left as it passes windswept trees to

Alternative route via Carperby

To visit Carperby take the right fork at Oxclose Gate and follow the leftward diagonally descending path, which in places is quite steep, into the village.

The Oxclose Road can be regained by taking the Leyburn road out of the village and turning left onto the first lane just beyond the village hall. Keep to the left of a small triangular green and where the lane folks take a rough, stony track leading off to the right (signposted Castle Bolton).

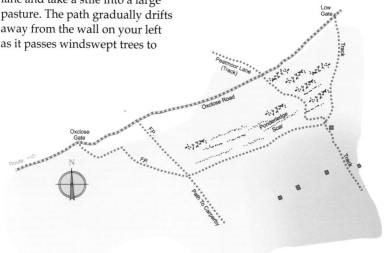

Carperby

Carperby is long, straggling village lying north of the River Ure on the old road between Hawes and Leyburn. Unlike many of its neighbours it has not yet succumbed to tourism or the holiday-cottage market. It is still very much a working village with a strong farming tradition going back to Saxon times.

Many of the surrounding fields, particularly the steeper slopes to the north of the village, have the appearance of corrugated paper. This is a characteristic of medieval strip cultivation where each holding was ploughed individually.

In the centre of the village is a 17th-century market cross set on seven square steps. Carperby was one of

The former Friends' Meeting House built in 1864

the first villages in Wensleydale to be granted a market charter in 1303.

Carperby like many Dales villages has a strong non-conformist Christian tradition. One of the finest buildings in the village is the former Friends' Meeting House built in 1864.

St Matthew's Well by the green has an impressive stone surround dated 1867.

The seven-stepped 17th-century market cross, Carperby

St Matthew's Well, Carperby

attain higher ground before falling away into a corner by a gate and stile. On your right the path coming up from Carperby joins the Oxclose bridleway. The views in all directions are superb. On the opposite side of the valley Penhill rises steeply above West Witton. Ahead in the middle distance stands our next

broad, green track which sweeps across a large, rough pasture below Locker Tarn. The track presents no navigational difficulties. At the far end of the pasture a stile alongside a gate admits to a rutted track which after 150 metres leads to a ford. Cross the beck and follow the broad track up a slight rise. The

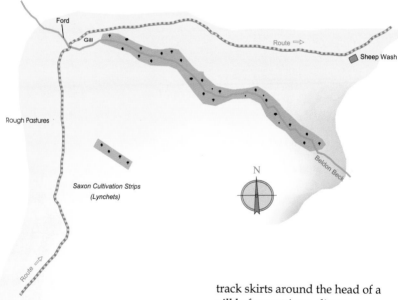

objective, Bolton Castle, occupying a broad terrace on the northern side of the River Ure. Take the stile and follow the

track skirts around the head of a gill before setting a direct course for Bolton Castle. All is now plain sailing. After passing through seven gates and to the left of farm buildings, the track terminates alongside the north-west tower of Bolton Castle.

Bolton Castle

Bolton Castle is considered to be the best surviving example of a 14th-century quadrangular castle. The castle was built for comfort rather than for its defensive qualities, which were limited. The site is overlooked by higher ground and there is no wet moat.

The castle was commissioned by Richard, Lord Scrope (pronounced "Scroop") in 1379 who came from a rich and powerful medieval family. The castle was completed in 1399 at a cost of £12,000. Lord Scrope was an eminent lawyer who under Richard II held the offices of Lord Chancellor and Lord Chief Justice

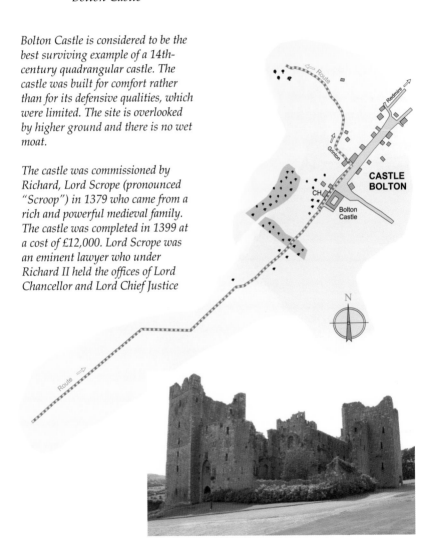

CASTLE BOLTON

CH

Bolton Castle

Bolton Castle was besieged by Oliver Cromwell in the Civil War. The siege weakened the north-east tower which collapsed during a storm in 1761.

of England.

The castle's most famous prisoner was Mary Queen of Scots who was held captive from 13 July 1568 to 26 January 1569.

Queen Mary's sojourn at Bolton Castle was not that of a typical prisoner whose lot was to be cast into a squalid, dank dungeon with no natural light. Mary had her own apartment in the south-west tower and was attended on by a retinue of

40 servants.

During the Civil War the castle, like many royalist strongholds across Yorkshire, took a heavy pounding from the parliamentary forces of Oliver Cromwell. After a siege lasting several months the royal garrison surrendered in 1645.

The north-east tower, which was severely weakened during the Civil War bombardment, collapsed during a storm in 1761.

Bolton Castle where Mary Queen of Scots was held captive for six months

Castle Bolton

Castle Bolton, the village, consists of a single street of neat, sandstone cottages with traditional gardens all bounded by a linear green and dominated at the far end by a massive medieval fortress. There is a simplicity about the village which greatly adds to its charm. Many of the cottages were formerly occupied by miners who worked the lead mines above the village.

Under the shadow of the castle walls stands the simple church of St Oswald's which was built about the same time as the castle.

There are so many picturesque cottages in Castle Bolton that to single one out is unfair on the others

The village pump

The Church of St Oswald's stands literally in the shadow of Bolton Castle. The simple church was built about the same time as the castle and is a perfect anti-dote to its mighty neighbour.

Distance: 4¾ miles (7.6km)

Walking Time: 2½ hours approximately

Terrain: Moderate to strenuous walking over rough pastures and exposed moorland. The section from Castle Bolton to the summit of Black Hill is unremittingly steep. The entire route crosses land where extensive lead mining has taken place in the past and where there are abandoned (unmarked and unfenced) mineshafts. At all times keep to the designated route or other public paths and bridleways. This section of the route should not be undertaken by inexperienced fellwalkers in winter, early spring or late autumn.

The route presents no navigational difficulties.

Map: 1:25 000 OS Explorer OL30−Yorkshire Dales−Northern and Central Areas

Route at a Glance:

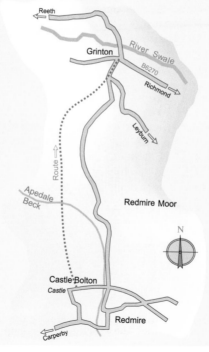

Route Overview: The route from Castle Bolton follows a steeply rising track onto semi-open moorland above the village and continues on a northerly course towards the summit of Black Hill. From Black Hill the route pursues the same course across open moorland to Dent's Houses and after crossing the watershed between Wensleydale and Swaledale reaches the summit of Greets Hill. From Greets Hill the route, on a falling-gradient path, heads towards Grinton passing a line of grouse butts before entering the village.

Accommodation: Grinton has a traditional inn with rooms close to the River Ure. Above the village, a youth hostel, Grinton Lodge, occupies a former shooting lodge. Reeth (less than a mile from Grinton) offers three traditional inns with rooms overlooking the green and several B&Bs..

Cafes and tea shops: Reeth

Public Houses: Grinton and Reeth

National Park Information Centre: Reeth

Village Shops: Reeth

Public Toilets: Reeth

Rail Services: The nearest main line stations to Grinton are (1) Darlington (24 miles away) on the East Coast Main Line and (2) Kirkby Stephen (also 24 miles away) on the Settle−Carlisle line.

Bus Services: A regular service operates between Richmond and Keld via Grinton and Reeth.

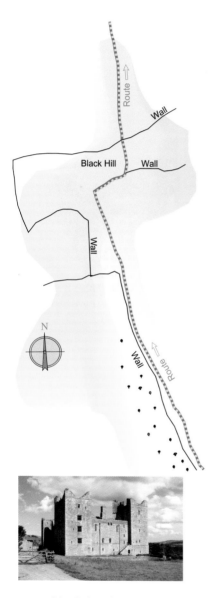

From Bolton Castle walk towards the village green. 150 metres from the castle a broad, stony track (signposted Grinton and Low Row) runs between two cottages on your left. Follow the rising track to a metal gate adjacent to a finger post marking a bridleway leading onto semi-open moorland above the village.

Cross a stream and bear half-left towards a wood and boundary wall. The path, which runs alongside the boundary wall, is exceptionally steep making for a heart pounding ascent of Black Hill. The views in retrospect provide some relief from the gruelling climb. On the opposite side of the valley Penhill, looking every inch a beacon fell, is the main focal point.

The shy, retiring side valley of Walden is immediately to the right of Penhill, and to the right of Walden is Bishopdale whose loyalties are divided between Wharfedale (where it has its head) and Wensleydale.

When you reach the corner of the boundary wall continue forward on the same line of ascent.

The path, now enclosed by two wire fences, inclines to the right

Bolton Castle seen from the west

before reverting to its former line of ascent. A stone wall crosses the path close to the summit of Black Hill. Take the squeeze-through stile and continue along the path towards the skyline. This is moorland walking par excellence.

The uphill path eventually relents and pursues a downhill course passing sheep enclosures prior to joining Apedale Road at Dent's Houses.

This is a land of nomenclature misnomers; houses are in reality barns or even sheep pens; roads are rough, unsurfaced moorland tracks; and primates do not inhabit the moors!

At the crossroads of moorland tracks take the uphill track which passes a line of grouse butts as it climbs towards the summit of Greets Hill.

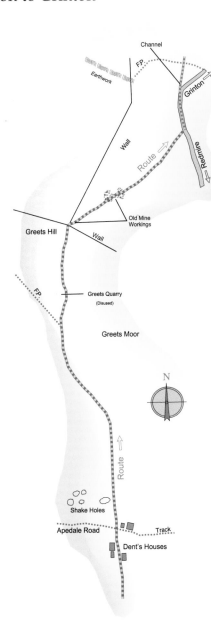

A horseshoe-shaped grouse butt

Ignore a minor path which joins
the main track from the left just
before an old quarry.

Greets Hill

*At 508 metres (1676ft) Greets Hill is
not the highest point en route to
Richmond but the views from the
summit cairn are, on a clear day, the
most far ranging of the entire walk.*

*In the north-east the Tees estuary
with its chemical and industrial
works fades imperceptibly into the
North Sea. The Cleveland Hills and
the Vale of York fill the eastern
prospect whilst the views to the south
are no less impressive with Penhill,
Great Whernside and Buckden Pike
providing the main focus of interest.
But the most poignant views are in
the far west where the faithful
landmarks of Penyghent,
Ingleborough and Whernside will not
be seen again on this walk.*

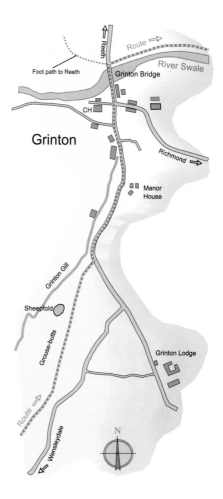

*A former shooting lodge at Grinton, now a youth
hostel*

From the north-eastern side of the cairn follow a rapidly deteriorating path towards and through a gate. The path is cairned and keeps to the right of grousebutts as it descends Greets Hill towards an unfenced moorland road. Follow the road with its wide, closely cropped grass verge down the hillside.

Vicarage Bridge, Grinton

At the commencement of the first right-hand bend in the road a grass strip marked by a finger post runs in a northerly direction along a channel. Follow the grass strip down the hillside crossing a broader track and keeping to the right of grouse butts. The path is not always

Swaledale seen from Greets Hill

obvious but if in doubt keep the parish church tower in your line of sight.

The views across the valley towards Reeth and Arkengarthdale are outstanding. Eventually the path is reunited with the moorland road via a corner field stile. Turn left and follow the steep road, now partnered by a fast flowing beck, into Grinton passing on the way some very old and attractive dwellings.

Grinton

Most villages in Swaledale lie on the sunnier north bank of the River Swale. Grinton is the exception: it lies on the shadier south bank. Grinton is a place of considerable antiquity predating the Norman Conquest. The oldest houses, dating from 1650, are built alongside the steep road to Leyburn which until the opening of the Reeth–Richmond turnpike in 1836 was the main route through the village.

The Parish Church of St Andrew's was originally early Norman though later additions have obliterated much of the original structure. The tower was rebuilt in 1500 and the church underwent a major restoration in 1896.

In medieval times the parish of Grinton was one of the largest in England. For hundreds of years Grinton had the only consecrated burial ground in Upper Swaledale. Corpses from higher up the dale were brought to Grinton for burial in wicker baskets by relays of men from each village.

The River Swale sweeping passed St Andrew's Church, Grinton

St Andrew's Church, Grinton, often referred to as "the Cathedral of the Dales"

The funeral procession along what became known as the Corpse Way could take several days. When the pallbearers and mourners needed a rest the wicker coffin would be placed on stone slabs purposely erected along the route. This medieval custom came to an end when a new church at Muker, a village higher up the dale, was built and a burial ground consecrated in 1580.

Reeth

Reeth, an attractive village less than a mile away from Grinton, is situated on a broad terrace above the confluence of the River Swale and Arkle beck. It is the largest village in Swaledale. Reeth's main asset is its large, sloping green set against a backdrop of dramatic fells, where a small market is held every Friday.

From Roman times lead has been mined in the hills above Reeth. The golden years of the lead industry were from 1670 to 1870 when mining brought prosperity to the village, reflected in the fine Georgian buildings built along the top of the green. Since its lead mining heyday the population of Reeth has declined by two-thirds. The lead mines have long since closed and tourism and farming are now the bedrock of the local economy.

Friday is market day in the Upper Swaledale village of Reeth

Distance: 9 ¼ miles (14.9km)

Walking Time: 5 hours approximately

Terrain: Easy to moderate walking throughout the route mainly along riverside paths, lower fellside terraces, through meadows, grazing pastures and wooded ravines, where exposed tree roots present a potential hazard in wet conditions.

Waymarking throughout the route is generally good.

Maps: (1) 1:25 000 OS Explorer OL30 – Yorkshire Dales – Northern & Central Areas and (2) 1:25 000 OS Explorer 304 – Darlington & Richmond

Route at a Glance:

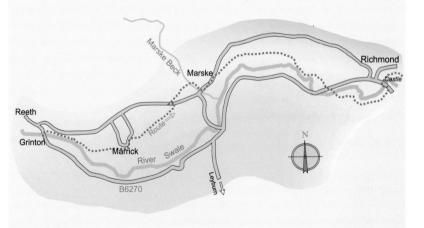

Route: From Grinton the route crosses the River Swale which it tracks downstream to Marrick Priory where it turns away from the river towards Marrick, a village situated on higher ground above the valley floor. From Marrick the route proceeds in a north-easterly direction towards Marske crossing Ellers Beck and passing to the west of Hutton's Monument. On joining the Reeth road above Marske the route takes a left turn before resuming its north-easterly course entering the village of Marske via Pillimire Bridge.

The route leaves Marske via the high road to Richmond before setting a course for Applegarth Scar. Below the scar the route joins a narrow fellside terrace which it follows eastwards to Low Applegarth where it changes course to rejoin the looping Swale. The route crosses the Swale at Round Howe and follows the river downstream through a wooded ravine to Richmond Bridge where a final crossing of the Swale is made. The route enters the town of Richmond via Cornforth Hill and terminates below the great keep of Richmond Castle.

Accommodation: Richmond offers a range of accommodation to suit most budgets ranging from the comfortable King's Head Hotel in the market place to simple B&Bs.

Cafes, restaurants and tea shops: Richmond

Public Houses: Richmond

Tourist Information Centre: Richmond

Post Office and Banks: Richmond

Public Toilets: Round Howe and Richmond

Rail Services: The nearest main line station to Richmond is Darlington (14 miles away) on the East Coast Line. .

Bus Services: A regular service operates between (1) Richmond, Grinton and Reeth (2) Richmond, Leyburn and Ripon (with onward connections to Harrogate and Leeds) and (3) Richmond and Darlington. Darlington is the nearest National Express Stop.

Calver Hill above Reeth seen from Grinton

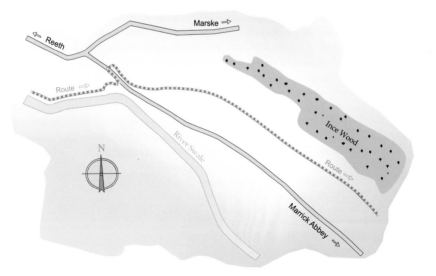

From the parish church walk to the road junction, bear left and cross the River Swale via the three-arched masonry bridge. Now turn right onto a riverside path which follows the Swale (the name means the whirling, rushing river) downstream. In late spring the riverside meadows are breathtakingly beautiful with millions of yellow buttercups gently sway in the breeze. On your left, overlooking the meadows, is a three-mile ridge of limestone scars known as

Fremmington Edge which is a popular destination for walkers based in Upper Swaledale.

After about 500 metres and a series of stiles, the path bears away from the river and enters a small, deciduous wood before joining a narrow road leading to Marrick Priory, our next objective. On reaching the road turn left and after 50 metres cross the first stile on your right. This leads into a large pasture whereupon bear half-right and

Marrick Priory, Swaledale

cross the pasture aiming for the south-west corner of Ince Wood. The path leads to a wooden stile backed by a wire fence. Cross the stile and follow the single-file path. The intermittently fading path follows a course which is roughly mid-way between the road on your right and Ince Wood on your left. Follow a line of stiles through a series of pastures with the tower of Marrick Priory becoming the main focal point ahead. Eventually the path terminates alongside a metal gate in the right-hand corner of the last pasture before a large farm. The right of way passes in front of the farm and Marick Priory.

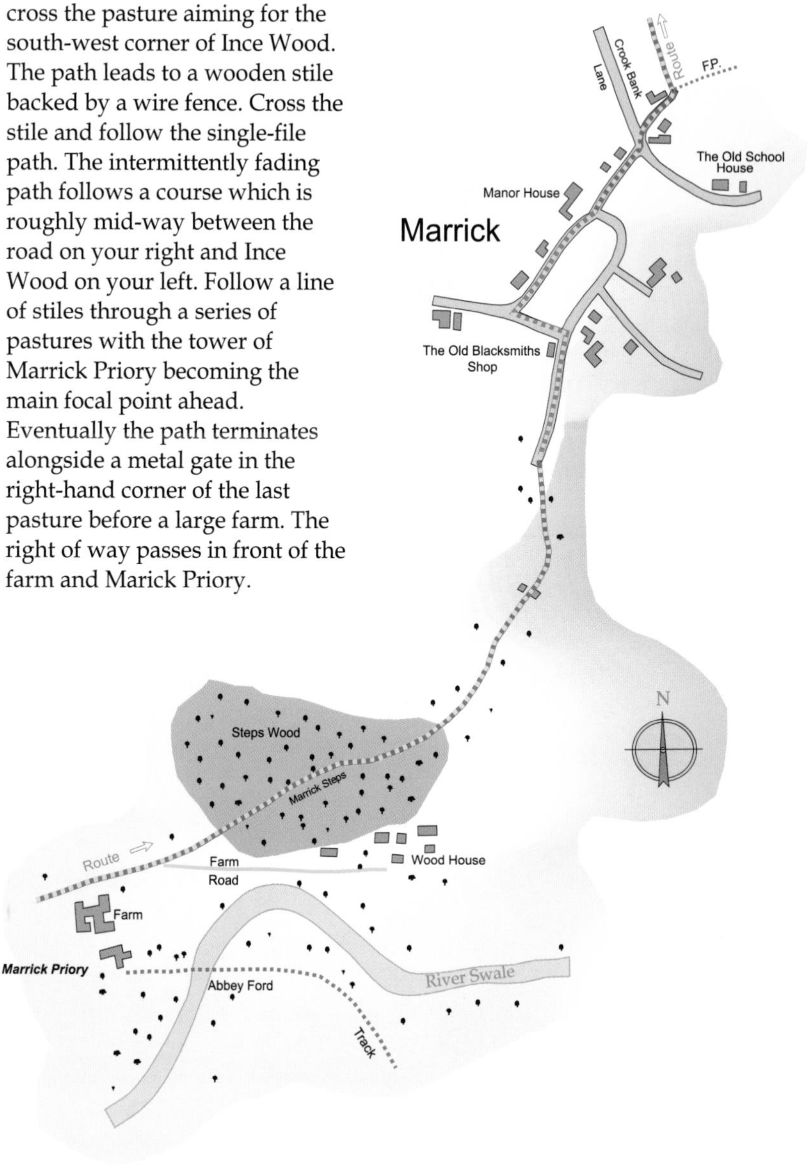

Crook Bank Lane

Route ⇨

F.P.

The Old School House

Manor House

Marrick

The Old Blacksmiths Shop

Steps Wood

Marrick Steps

N

Route ⇨

Farm Road

Wood House

Farm

Marrick Priory

Abbey Ford

River Swale

Track

The old priory is not open to the public but visitors may walk down the drive to see the remains of the east window.

Marrick Priory

Marrick Priory was founded in 1154 for Benedictine nuns. The nunnery was one of the wealthiest in Yorkshire though still poor by the standard of male monastic houses. Henry VIII dissolved the priory in 1539. At the time of dissolution the priory had 12 black robed nuns overseen by a prioress.

Of the original buildings only the tower remains intact. Parts of the priory church, the prioress's house and refectory have been incorporated into later building works.

One mile downstream from Marrick Priory, on the opposite bank of the Swale, lies the remains of a Cistercian nunnery. Only the 15th-century tower has survived. The Cistercian nuns wore white robes and unlike their talkative sisters across the river were a silent order.

A short distance beyond the drive leading to the priory a finger post on your left marks the path to Marrick village. Pass through the gate and follow the green, slanting path as it climbs gently towards Steps Wood. The path affords splendid retrospective views of the priory and surrounding fells.

Enter Steps Wood via a wicket gate. The name of the wood is apposite for there are reputedly 375 stone steps through the ancient wood. The stone "causey" has deteriorated since it

The 15th-century tower is all that remains of a Cistercian nunnery

A leaded glass and sandstone window –Marrick Priory

was laid down for use by nuns in the medieval period.

Exit the wood through a gate that leads into an open field with superb views of Lower Swaledale. The well-trodden path runs parallel to a stone wall on your right before emerging in front of a metal gate leading onto a broad track bordered by two stone barns. Follow the track, ignoring the path on your right, through a second metal gate and walk forward onto a surfaced road passing on your left a former Wesley Chapel and on your right a second ecclesiastical

Two charming cottages in Marrick, one with an interesting sundial

building serving a new role. When you reach the road junction turn left and then right at the second junction. Walk forward passing on your left two charming old cottages, one with an interesting sundial. Continue along the main street of the village passing on your left a telephone box.

At the point where the road sweeps round a corner on leaving the village turn right onto an access lane. Follow the lane passing on your left the old village school and school house. A few steps further on a finger post directs to Hollins Farm. Leave the lane at this juncture and follow a broad, stony track on your left. The track soon funnels into a well-trodden, single-file path as it passes across a number of small enclosures on the edge of the village before making a right diagonal crossing of a large, downhill sloping pasture.

Ancient Steps Wood replete with stone "causey"

Marrick

Marrick today is a peaceful farming community having long ago made the transition from mining and smelting of lead which from the 16th to the 19th-century dominated the village. Lead has been mined here since Roman times.

A notable feature of the village is its spaciousness with most houses having unusually large gardens and orchards.

At 304 metres (997ft) above sea level the village is one of the highest (and coldest!) in Swaledale.

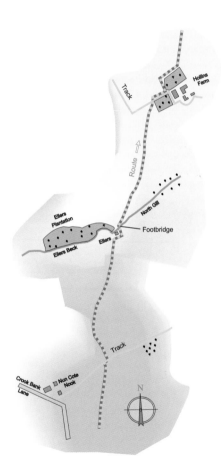

If you crave for the company of fellow walkers then this section of the walk is unlikely to disappoint as it is shared with coast to coasters who in summer, especially mid-morning, form a congo-like procession as they head across the fields to Marske.

The farm on your left, depending on the time of day and season, serves refreshments to coast to coasters, or indeed anyone in need of sustenance.

In the middle distance an obelisk

marks the grave of Matthew
Hutton, a wealthy landowner
who lived at Marske Hall and
who died in 1814.

Pass through a metal gate, turn
right on meeting the farm access
road and after 30 metres bear
sharp left and continue towards a
barn where a metal gate leads
into a broad, sloping pasture.
Now make a right diagonal
crossing of the pasture keeping

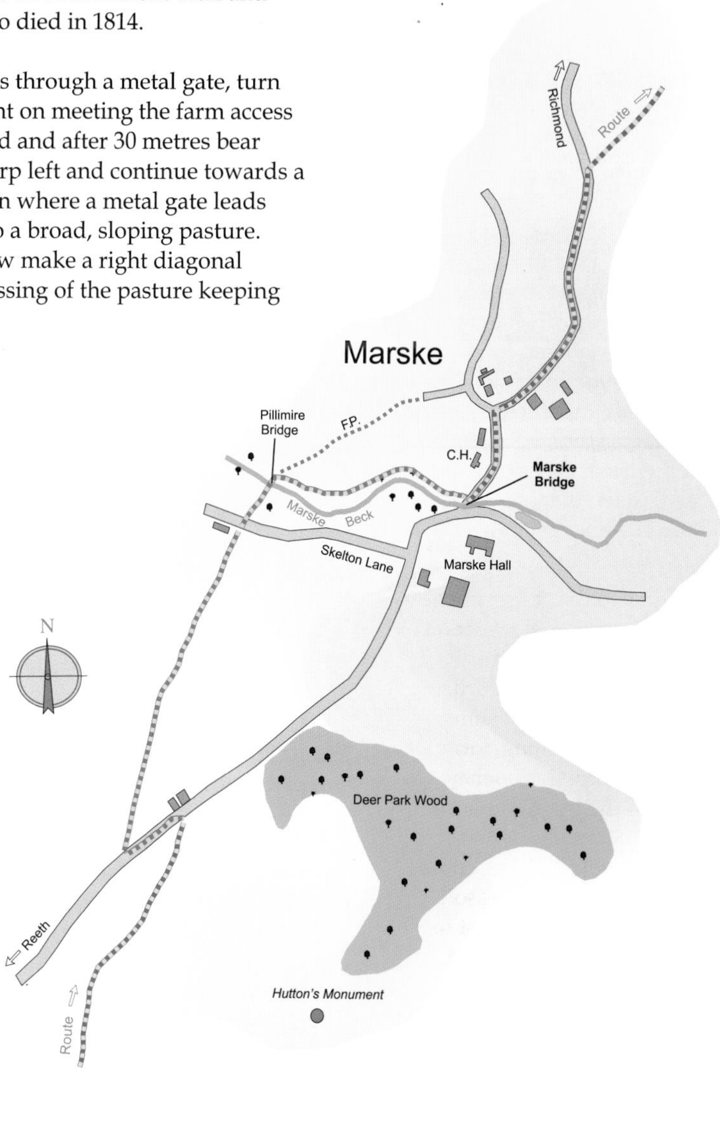

Richmond

Route

Marske

Pillimire
Bridge

F.P.

C.H.

**Marske
Bridge**

Marske Beck

Skelton Lane

Marske Hall

N

Deer Park Wood

Reeth

Route

Hutton's Monument

the cottage in your line of sight.
Pass in front of the cottage which
takes the name Ellers (derived
from the word *alders*) from a
nearby beck. To the side of the
cottage a small gate leads to a
footbridge that crosses Ellers
beck. After the footbridge make a
right diagonal crossing of two
further pastures emerging at a
gate alongside the access road to
Hollins Farm. Pass through the
gate, turn right and after 100
metres, just before the farm
entrance, turn left and follow a
stone wall round to a stile. There
is a plethora of unofficial
waymarks to guide you safely
round the farm! Cross the stile
and make a left diagonal crossing
of the field above the farm. Now
take a second stile and follow a
stone wall leading to a finger post

Ellers Cottage, a well-known landmark on the Coast to Coast Walk

by a metal gate. Go through the
gate and locate a farmhouse,
encircled by a belt of trees lying
on a north-easterly bearing. Aim
for the farmhouse which, though
not apparent from this distance,
lies on the opposite side of the
Marske road. As you advance
you should notice a stile leading
onto the road. Cross the stile,
turn left and walk up the road
until you reach a finger post on
your right (less than 200 metres).
Go through a metal gate into a
pasture, with no sign of a visible
path, and proceed half-right
picking out as you advance the
first of two stiles. After the
second stile locate a house lying
at the foot of the steeply sloping
pasture. Initially aim for the
house but as you advance divert
to a stile slightly to the right of
the house. The stile admits to a
tarmac lane. Cross the lane and
proceed through a gate into a
small field dominated by a

A barn door in need of a lick of paint

magnificent willow tree. The secluded valley you are now entering encapsulates in miniature the finest characteristics of the Dales' landscape: isolated farmsteads, historic halls, sparkling becks, riverside meadows, ancient woodlands, open moors, dry stone walls, and yet, incredibly, this lovely valley lies outside the Yorkshire Dales National Park!

Pass to the left of the willow tree. Ahead is an interesting bridge with two segmental arches – one bridging Marske Beck, the other over dry land. The bridge is called Pillimire and dates from the 18th century; it probably was used by packhorses carrying lead

A waterwheel alongside Marske Beck

ore. After crossing the bridge you are confronted by two official paths. Take the lower path which follows the beck downstream as it passes through semi-open water meadows. After a short distance the path enters a tree-shaded stretch of river before emerging at Marske Bridge built in the 15th-century and a strong contender for the title of oldest

Pillimire Bridge, Marske

bridge in the Dales. Climb the steps on the left-hand side of the bridge and on reaching the road via a stile turn left. Now walk forward passing on your right ornamental gardens, constructed in 1836, and on your left, partially hidden behind dense foliage, St Edmund's Church.

Marske, the name is derived from the word "marsh"

Marske

The sheltered village of Marske lies in a lovely side dale drained by a charming beck. The village is in total harmony with its idyllic setting with each building reposing gracefully against a backdrop of wooded, rolling hills and wild moors.

During the Middle Ages Marske was a settlement of foresters and huntsmen but it was lead and coal

mining that came to dominate the village until these industries fell into decline and farming gained the ascendancy.

Marske and the name Hutton are synonymous. Matthew Hutton acquired the manor in 1597 and two of his descendants had strong ecclesiastical leanings, one becoming Archbishop of York and another

Marske Hall

Archbishop of Canterbury.

Another member of the Hutton dynasty whose passion was horse racing rather than matters spiritual is buried on a hill south of the village. His grave is marked by a 18.3 metres (60ft) obelisk.

The church, dedicated to St Edmund a Saxon King and Saint put to death by the Danes in AD 870, is 12th-century though much rebuilding took place in the 17th-century. The inside of the church is more interesting than its rather crude exterior. There are unusually painted box pews with one facing the chancel set aside for the Hutton family.

St Edmund's Church has its origins in the 12th-century and invites exploration

At the junction bear right, follow the road for 500 metres and leave the road via a stile on your right marked by a finger post. Now make a left diagonal crossing of four pastures initially aiming for a small plantation of trees. The path is barely visible. Leave the fourth pasture via a stile which crosses a wire fence.

Maintaining the same course, follow the path as it descends via steps into a lightly wooded gill through which flows Clapgate Beck. Cross the beck via a footbridge and climb out of the gill on a rightward-slanting path which passes below electricity lines carried on tall wooden pylons.

Continue along the thin-hillside path as it advances towards a limestone cairn situated below Applegarth Scar. The cairn marks the point where the path joins a farm access track contouring below Applegarth Scar. Turn right and follow the track towards West Applegarth

Farm. The views all around are exquisite. The looping Swale passes silently down the valley and rising above the riverside meadows are conical-shaped hills topped with trees. Higher up the fellside outcrops of shattered limestone glisten in the midday sun.

The gently descending farm track, now bordered by yew trees, passes in front of West Applegarth Farm with its elaborate chimney pots and lovely old stone mullion windows. Just beyond the farmhouse the path forks. Ignore the left-hand branch as this leads into Deep Dale above the limestone scars. Instead keep to the main track which passes to the right of a derelict barn where it narrows to a single-file path.

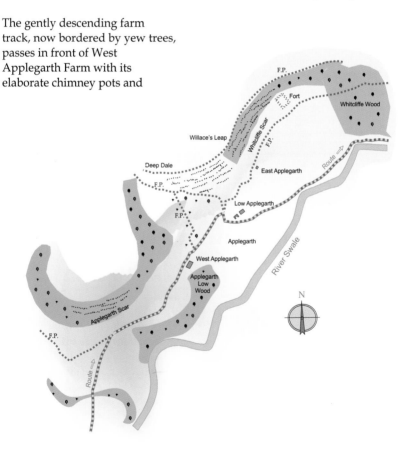

A limestone cairn below Applegarth Scar

Sheep are the lifeblood of the Dales' hill farmer

After crossing two pastures pause in front of a squeeze-through stile (signposted Coast to Coast). Now turn round 180 degrees. On your left a derelict stone wall runs down the rough pasture away from Low Applegarth Farm. Follow the derelict stone wall which leads to a cart track accessing the farm. Cross the track and aim for a stile next to a metal gate. Take the stile and follow a stone wall on your left for 30 metres before turning left through an open gateway into a large pasture. Make a right diagonal crossing of the pasture passing close to electricity pylons and in front of a derelict barn standing in the left-hand corner of the pasture. Cross over a stile into the next pasture and continue along the broad, green path until you reach the riverbank.

The views across the valley are unfortunately marred by a static caravan park sited on the opposite bank of the river. Now follow the river downstream over two stiles. The walk along the river bank even in the depths of winter is an absolute joy.

The official right of way bears away from the riverbank and enters Whitecliffe Wood. Ignore the official path (which in any event is easily missed) in favour of a permissive path which

Richmond Bridge built in the 1780s has inspired many artists including JMW Turner

continues close to the riverbank until a loop in the river blocks further progress. At this point head towards a large metal gate leading into Whitecliffe Wood and follow a rough cart track through the wood. Leave the wood via a stile. The track leads to a gate where a waymarked diversion directs walkers round the back of Lowenthwaite Farm. The diversion runs alongside a conifer hedge and ends at a stile on your right admitting to a green lane below a farm gate. Turn left and follow the lane to the main road. As you approach the road the 12th-century keep of Richmond Castle, our final

objective, comes into view for the first time.

On the opposite side of the road a gap in a low stone wall leads to a woodland path that follows the Swale downstream to Round Howe car park. At the far end of the car park turn right onto a footbridge. Cross the Swale

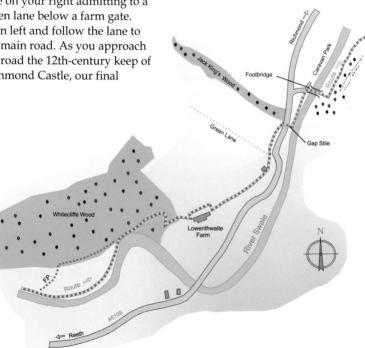

keeping a lookout for kingfishers and herons which frequent this stretch of the river.

Turn left immediately on reaching the end of the bridge and proceed through a wooden gate and follow the riverside path. When the path divides take the right branch which bears away from the river towards higher ground. (It is advisable not to take the riverside path which is impassable and dangerous when the river is running high.) After crossing a stile follow a broad, green track

Round Howe

Round Howe is a conical-shaped tree-covered hill formed during the last Ice Age. The River Swale originally flowed round the south side of the Howe but melting ice waters scoured out a new channel on the opposite side creating an isolated hill. The old south channel was filled in by glacial deposits.

The tree-shaded Swale at Round Howe

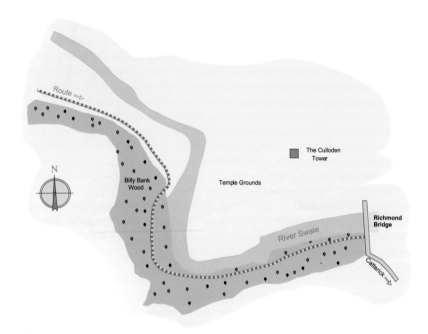

towards Billy Bank Wood. The path climbs steadily through the intriguingly named wood where copper was once mined. The woodland path affords splendid views of the river far below.

On exiting the wood turn left and cross Richmond Bridge. This famous 18th-century bridge, designed by the great Yorkshire architect, John Carr (Harewood House and Constable Burton Hall were also designed by Carr) was the start of the Richmond to Lancaster turnpike. The bridge,

particularly in winter and early spring before the trees above the riverbank add their foliage, provides a good view of Richmond Castle which occupies a commanding position high above the river. Walk forward onto Bridge Street passing on your left The Green lined with picturesque old stone cottages.

In medieval times this area was the home of various guilds engaged in tanning, brewing and milling. Overlooking The Green is the Culloden Tower, a grand

and imposing Georgian folly.

A cottage standing on the north-eastern corner of The Green bearing the date 1689 above its door has two Georgian sundials on its south and east facing walls dating from 1720.

From The Green proceed up the hill and after 100 metres turn right into Cornforth Hill, an historic street lined with charming cottages whose light, stone walls are adorned in summer with old-fashioned climbing roses.

Pass under a stone arch which in the medieval period was an

The 18th-century Culloden Tower

The Culloden Tower

The Culloden Tower was commissioned in 1746 by a wealthy Yorkshire parliamentarian, John Yorke, to commemorate the Duke of Cumberland's victory over the Scots at Culloden.

It stands on the site of a fortified tower built in the reign of Edward II by William de Huddeswell to protect the occupants from the threat of Scottish raids.

Historic Cornforth Hill

The 14th-century Postern Gate separating Cornforth Hill from the Bar

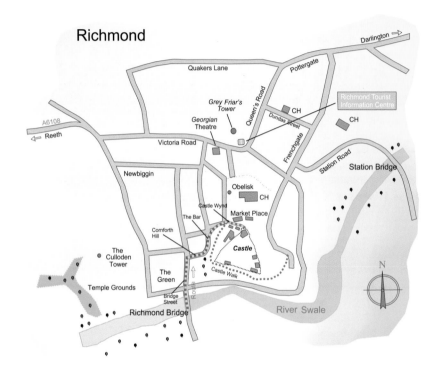

important gateway allowing access to the fortified town. Vestiges of the defensive walls built in the 14th-century to protect Richmond from Scottish raids are still evident. From the gateway bear left into a narrow, cobbled passageway known as the Bar. On reaching the top of the Bar turn right into New Road and after few a paces bear right into Castle Wynd (many narrow passageways in Richmond bear the name of *wynd*) which leads directly to the entrance of the castle. Our walk to Richmond started in the shadow of a great medieval fortress and fittingly we end the journey as it began.

Richmond lying at the foot of Swaledale in North Yorkshire does not entirely conform with the features and characteristics normally associated with a north country market town. The town looks as if it has been transplanted from a foreign land – France, possibly, or even Spain. The huge, cobbled market place, the largest in England, has a distinctly continental feel.

This continental feel extends to street names such as Frenchgate "the street of Franks"; and the name of Richmond is derived from the old French words "rich" and "mont" meaning strong hill.

Standing on an island site in the centre of the market place is Holy Trinity Church which must be the only church in the world with a regimental museum under its north aisle.

Richmond is something of a Middle Ages upstart. It came into existence when William the Conqueror granted his second cousin, Alan Rufus (who fought

The historic town of Richmond is dominated by a great Norman keep

alongside William at the Battle of Hastings and later brutally suppressed northern opposition to William's reign) one of the largest feudal holdings in England. Alan Rufus set about building a new town from scratch, the Middle Ages equivalent of a Milton Keynes, centred on a new, stone castle built on a promontory above the Swale.

The great Norman keep

The Castle

Richmond castle is one of the oldest stone built castles in England dating from 1071, though work on the rectangular keep did not begin until 1146. The keep is over 30 metres

(98ft) high and in relation to its ground area the tallest in England.

The castle not being on a strategically important route was never tested by a prolonged siege, played no part in the Wars of the Roses nor in the Civil War of the 17th-century.

The castle and its grounds are in the care of English Heritage and open to visitors at set times throughout the year.

Elegant Georgian town houses in Newbiggin

Georgian Richmond

During the 18th-century Richmond developed into a fashionable town in which the professional and merchant classes built themselves elegant townhouses. The market place though medieval in layout and a hotchpotch of undistinguished, modern retail facades contains many attractive Georgian buildings, including the King's Head Hotel and the Town Hall.

The market cross standing on a stepped pedestal is not actually a cross at all but an obelisk with a ball on top. It was erected in 1771.

Newbiggin, a delightfully pleasant, spacious, tree-lined street with a cobbled square, is bordered by handsome Georgian town houses.

Frenchgate, which originally housed the Breton supporters of Earl Alan and his descendants, is lined with charming, tall Georgian houses.

Another Georgian gem, though not its bland exterior, is the beautifully restored and unique Theatre Royal in Victoria Road. It was built in 1788 by actor-manager Samuel Butler.

The 15th-century Grey Friar's Tower, arguably one of the most graceful structures in the north of England

Grey Friar's Tower

Grey Friar's Tower in Friary Gardens opposite the Theatre Royal is all that remains above ground of a Franciscan Friary founded around 1258. The graceful, perpendicular Gothic-style bell tower was built in the 15th-century.

The 12th-century Holy Trinity Church is now the home of the Green Howards Regimenal Museum

*Richmond in Yorkshire predates all
other towns of the same name*

A charming corner of Richmond

The cobbled market square is the largest in England

The Obelisk with the ball on top was erected in 1771 and replaced the town's ancient market cross

The genesis of the walk described in this guidebook can be traced to the military ambitions of a great Roman general who ruled Britain nearly 2,000 years ago. Julius Agricola was consolidating his hold on the conquered territories of northern Britain by building a series of permanent fortifications at Lancaster, Ribchester and along the Lune Valley. On the eastern side of the Pennines Agricolan forts were being built at Catterick (near Richmond), Bainbridge and along the eastern fringe of the Yorkshire Dales.

The Pennines, a forbidding, vast tract of poorly drained, windswept moorland and fells inhabited by bears and wolves, formed a natural barrier between Lancashire and Yorkshire and from where the native Celtic tribes mounted a guerilla-type campaign against the Roman invaders. To crush Celtic resistance and protect his important trade routes (lead mined in the Yorkshire Dales was used to roof cathedrals in Roman Europe) Agricola ordered his engineers to build a military road over the Pennines linking his forts in Lancashire with those in Yorkshire.

The military road from Lancashire to Yorkshire was completed around AD 80 and, apart from a short section between Lancaster and Ingleton, still survives mostly as a rough track worn down to its bedrock – not surprising after almost 2,000 years of use.

During the turbulent Dark Ages the Roman Road across the Pennines would have been used by waves of Angles, Danes and Vikings on their migratory route across the central Pennines. In the Middle Ages the old road developed into a packhorse route for transporting coal, lead, iron ore, salt, corn, wool and various other commodities between Lancashire and Yorkshire. By 1720 this high-level route was known as the Devil's Causeway, an apt name for such a mysterious, lonely and bleak highway.

But it was in the mid-18th century that the old military road was given a new lease of life with the rise of Lancaster as a major west coast port. A new turnpike road was built between Lancaster and Richmond which effectively became a coast to coast route. Richmond was connected by road with the town of Yarm, a prosperous port on the tidal Tees a few miles south-east of Darlington. Thus merchandise could be shipped from the West Indies and the American colonies, unloaded at Lancaster, transported by horse-drawn wagons across the Pennines, reloaded at Yarm for onward shipment to ports bordering the North Sea.

Appendix Two:
Geology of The Yorkshire Dales

The following is a brief description of the main geological features found in the Yorkshire Dales.

Limestone

Limestone is made of sediments that have settled on the seabed over millions of years. Three hundred million years ago most of the Yorkshire Dales were covered by a shallow tropical sea inhabited by billions of small filter-feeding sea creatures. Sea water contains dissolved lime which the filter feeders extracted. The limey bones and shells of these creatures settled on the seabed and over time were compressed into limestone by the weight of mud (which turns to shale) and sand (which turns to sandstone) washed down by rivers into the sea. This cycle was repeated many times over millions of years as layers of limestone, shale and sandstone were formed.

Limestone Pavements

During the past two million years there have been at least three periods of glaciation affecting the Dales, the last one beginning 80,000 years ago. As the ice advanced it stripped the softer rock and soil cover exposing the much harder limestone underneath leaving a flat surface of bare rock. Subsequent erosion of the pavement by wind, rainwater and frost action has created the present landscape.

Grikes

Grikes are the deep clefts that break up limestone pavements and give them a fractured appearance. Grikes have their own micro-climate and being moist and rich in lime and protected from nibbling sheep provide ideal conditions for plant growth –wood anemone, hart's-tongue fern, spleenwort, wild garlic and occasionally rare plants can be found.

Scars

Scars are made of a thick layer of shattered limestone which has been undercut by an advancing glacier. Twisleton Scars on the north side of Chapel-le-Dale and Raven Scar on the opposite side of the valley are classic examples of ice cutting deep into the limestone rock and creating a "U" shaped valley.

Shake Holes

Shake holes (also called swallow holes) are a common feature of limestone country; they are funnel-shaped hollows formed where water has seeped into joints and cracks in the limestone rock below causing the limestone to dissolve and the ground above to collapse.

Caves and Potholes

Caves and potholes are formed where slightly acidic surface water has flowed or percolated through cracks in the limestone rock until a drainage route is established, thus enabling dissolved material to be washed away leaving a labyrinth of connecting passages and caves.

Erratics

Erratics are boulders standing on a narrow pedestal of rock above the limestone pavement. They are a relic of the last Ice Age having been plucked from their source, usually many miles away, by an advancing wall of ice and dumped out of situ when the ice melted. Many erratics can be seen on Scales Moor between Ingleton and Ribblehead.

Drumlins

Drumlins are smooth rounded hillocks, typically 500 metres long comprising small stones and clay with a rock core, formed during the final stages of glaciation. Their alignment indicates the direction in which the ice flowed. Ribblehead has the region's highest concentration of drumlins.

Appendix Three:
Useful Information

Tourist Information

www.touristinformationcentres.com
www.information-britain.co.uk
www.yorkshiredales.org

Lancaster Tourist Information
The Storey
Meeting House Lane
Lancaster LA1 1TH
01524 582394

www. visitlancaster.co.uk

Ingleton Tourist Information
The Community Centre Car Park
Main Street
Ingleton
Carnforth LA6 3HG
015242 41049

Richmond Tourist Information Centre
Friary Gardens
Victoria Road
Richmond
North Yorkshire DL10 4AJ
01748 850252

Yorkshire Dales National Park Centres

Aysgarth Falls National Park Centre
Aysgarth Falls
Aysgarth
North Yorkshire DL8 3TH
01969 662910

Hawes National Park Centre
Station Yard
Hawes
North Yorkshire DL8 3NT
01969 666210

Reeth National Park Centre
Literary Institute
Reeth
North Yorkshire DL11 6TE
01748 884059

Travel

www.nationalrail.co.uk
www.thetrainline.com
www.traveline.co.uk
www.nationalexpress.com
www.yorkshiretravel.net
www.traveldales.org.uk
www.dalesbus.org
www.wensleydalerailway.com

Walking Associations

Ramblers' Association
2nd Floor Camelford House
87-90 Albert Embankment
London SE1 7TW
0207 339 8500
www.ramblers.org.uk

Youth Hostel Association
www.yha.org.uk

Youth hostels on or close to the route
Ingleton, Grinton and Hawes

Mountain Rescue
Dial 999 and request *Police*

Weather

www.metoffice.gov.uk
www.bbc.co.uk/weather

Outdoor Market Days (selected)

Tuesday: Hawes and Settle
Wednesday: Lancaster, Bentham and Northallerton
Thursday: Kirkby Lonsdale
Friday: Ingleton, Leyburn and Reeth
Saturday: Lancaster, Northallerton and Richmond

Appendix Four:
Countryside Code

There are five sections of The Countryside Code (July 2004 edition) dedicated to helping members of the public respect, protect and enjoy the countryside. The five sections are:

Be safe, plan ahead and follow any signs

Leave gates and property as you find them

Protect plants and animals and take your litter home

Keep dogs under close control

Consider other people

The full code can be downloaded by visiting http://www.countrysideaccess.gov.uk and follow the links.